PRADISE FOR

The Desire Factor

"*The Desire Factor* is a testament to the success principles I've been living and teaching for more than forty years. Whether we experience happiness or unhappiness, success or failure depends on what we, ourselves, believe we are deserving of. What we think about, talk about, feel strongly about, and act on, we attract into our lives. In this book, my friend Christy Whitman lays out a reliable road map for how to do all of the above on purpose."

—Jack Canfield, coauthor of the #1 *New York Times* bestselling Chicken Soup for the Soul® series and *The Success Principles*™, and a featured teacher in *The Secret*

"In *The Desire Factor*, Christy Whitman has pulled back the curtain and revealed how successful people fulfill their desires. Well-written, with engaging, easy-to-relate-to stories, this book will guide you to a completely new understanding of what fulfilling desires means and why you have the desires you have. This is one of those books to put on your must-read list."

—Chris Attwood, *New York Times* bestselling author of *The Passion Test* and *Your Hidden Riches*

"As a TM meditator of almost forty years, I've often felt profoundly connected to our collective quantum soup. Christy Whitman's *The Desire Factor* beautifully makes the case that desire not only doesn't deserve its bad rap (thanks a lot, Adam and Eve), but it's actually one of the soup's most transformational ingredients."

—Tom Bergeron, TV host and soup resident

"*The Desire Factor* is a handbook that teaches you how to manifest any desire, big or small. Christy reveals the art and science of creating fulfillment and empowerment in every aspect of your life. Bravo, Christy, for sharing these important principles."

—Cynthia Kersey, bestselling author of *Unstoppable*, founder & CEO of Unstoppable Foundation

"*The Desire Factor* is a must-read for anyone wanting to create an incredible life. The seven-step process in this book demonstrates what you must do to have anything you desire—and ultimately become the person you have always wanted to be."

—T. Harv Eker, #1 *New York Times* bestselling author of *Secrets of the Millionaire Mind*™

"*The Desire Factor* powerfully speaks to a new paradigm for the manifestation of our worldly hopes and dreams. It not only enhances traditional meditation and visualization techniques, but it also activates your direct experience of the energy source of all manifestation. Once you know how to connect with this energy, you can direct it toward creating any outcome you desire and live the life you were meant to live. Well done, Christy."

—Dr. Sue Morter, #1 bestselling author of *The Energy Codes*

"*The Desire Factor* is a must-read for anyone seeking to become a more deliberate creator of their own life experience. Christy Whitman breaks down how to change any circumstance by changing the energy we bring to it. Her seven-step process of alignment, focus, joyful expectancy, having, loving, surrender, and action demonstrates the adjustments we must make in our energy in order to magnetize any outcome we desire."

—Michael Bernard Beckwith, founder and spiritual director of Agape International Spiritual Center, author of *Life Visioning* and *Spiritual Liberation*

"Let your burning desires set the world on fire and let Christy Whitman's *The Desire Factor* light the way."

—Mike Dooley, *New York Times* bestselling author of *Infinite Possibilities*

"Most of us interact with life as mere shadows of who we really are. We continue to tell the same tired stories about what's happened to us in the past, and we drag around perceptions and belief systems that oppose the very outcomes we want. *The Desire Factor* breaks down the process of how each of us creates the reality we are living, and guides readers expertly through the art and science of shifting one's point of attraction. The result is a reawakening to the truth of who each of us truly is at our core: powerful, energetic beings who have the ability to shape and reshape our destiny in every moment in time."

—Lisa Nichols, *New York Times* bestselling author and featured teacher in *The Secret*

"Desire is at the root of our humanity. Desire for life. Desire for abundance. Desire for love. Without desire, there is nothing to drive our progress as a species. Still, there is a stigma and misunderstanding around desire, which prevents people from allowing themselves to experience a life they would truly love. Christy shines her brilliant light on our current ideas about desire and how we learn to not only allow desire but also thrive on it. She shares her years of experience with manifesting and the Law of Attraction as well so that you learn not only about the role of desire in your life but also how to realize those desires."

—Bob Doyle, featured expert in *The Secret*

"Christy Whitman has done an amazing job! *The Desire Factor* takes you on an inspiring journey. Christy has created a must-read in the self-help category! Anyone suffering from frustration, overwhelm, or anxiety needs to read *The Desire Factor* and keep it in their reference library."

—Dave Pratt, radio personality, ABA Hall of Fame,
Music & Entertainment Hall of Fame

"*The Desire Factor* guides you through the essential internal steps you must take to attract anything you desire in the external world. Both scientifically sound and easy to understand, Christy Whitman's book leads you to the understanding that the universe is always listening, interacting, and responding. An empowering, must-read book for anyone seeking to reclaim their power to attract what they desire on purpose."

—Dr. Joe Vitale, star of *The Secret*, author of *The Attractor Factor*
and *The Miracle*

"To magnetize anything you desire into your life—whether it's financial prosperity, freedom of self-expression in your career, or living happily ever after with your soul mate—your energy must be in resonant alignment with whatever outcome you want to receive. *The Desire Factor* not only shows you how to manifest the things you desire but also reveals the formula for being joyful in the meantime."

—Arielle Ford, author of *The Soulmate Secret*

"*The Desire Factor* is about so much more than manifesting your desires. It is a handbook for strengthening your connection with the all-powerful presence that created you and that oversees the flow of all things. From the information and processes presented throughout this book, you will learn how to manifest any desire, big or small. But more important, you will learn the art and science of aligning your own energy, and this is the key to finding fulfillment and empowerment in every aspect and circumstance of your life."

—Natalie Ledwell, bestselling author and cofounder of Mind Movies

"What an incredibly leading-edge healer and channeler Christy Whitman is! Thank you for blessing us with this treasure map to our Desire Factor!"

—Jason Stephenson, manager of Relax Me Online Australia

"Sirians are elated to see humans on Earth now claiming and embodying the fifth-dimensional awareness! As you tune in to the energetic coding of this book, tuning in to the Light emissions of Christy and the Council, you will discover *The Desire Factor* is a higher elevation attunement instrument . . . not just a book. It is, in fact, a proof that humanity has accelerated into 5D."

—Athella, Sirius B

"*The Desire Factor* is essential for everyone to read no matter how big or small your desires are, and no matter what they are! Anyone who wants to learn how to go from an idea to fulfillment of that idea *must* read *The Desire Factor!*"

—JJ Virgin, *New York Times* bestselling author of *The Virgin Diet*

"Your dreams and heartfelt desires serve a very high spiritual purpose. They provide a powerful catalyst to reach for more, to expand past self-imposed limitations, and to become the person you have always wanted to be. *The Desire Factor* provides a clear, step-by-step blueprint for manifesting any desire, big or small, and for realizing your greatest potential."

—Sage Lavine, author and founder of Women Rocking Business

"Desire is an important part of the creation process, and *The Desire Factor* is the road map for that divine creation process. Christy Whitman does an outstanding job of guiding the reader step by step through the process of creating what you desire in your life. This is so leading edge and a must-read for any spiritual seeker."

—Jennifer Hough, expert in the physics of flow, president of the Wide Awakening

"We all know we are spiritual beings having a temporary human experience. *The Desire Factor* teaches us how to make the most of the human, material plane of reality as we simultaneously align with the infinite spirits we are. A fine line indeed . . . and Christy will show you how to walk it . . . in designer shoes, looking and feeling fabulous every step of the way. Her seven-step process of alignment, focus, joyful expectancy, having, loving, surrender, and action demonstrates exactly how to take a desire to its fulfillment."

—Kelly Sullivan Walden, bestselling author of *It's All in Your Dreams*
and *Dream Goddess Empowerment Deck*

"Your desires serve a divine purpose. They provide an avenue for you to realize your power as a divine creator. Christy Whitman brilliantly shares the principles to get you to your desires with ease, grace, and flow. *The Desire Factor* provides a clear, step-by-step guidepost for manifesting any desire and for realizing your divine potential. This is a must-read!"

—Gina DeVee, author of *The Audacity to Be Queen*, founder of Divine Living

"Christy Whitman has nailed it. *The Desire Factor* is a must-read for anyone wanting to create success and who wants to fully understand the power of the process."

—Ali Brown, entrepreneur mentor, founder of The Trust

"Our perception of how the universe operates is rapidly changing. Where we once believed hard work and sacrifice to be the path to success, we now understand that perception, attitude, and vibration are the powerful internal forces that account for a big part of achieving the success we desire. In *The Desire Factor*, Law of Attraction coach Christy Whitman explains the vibrational nature of all things in language that is easy to understand, and she provides a powerful formula to follow for the manifestation of any desire."

—John Assaraf, *New York Times* bestselling author of *The Answer* and *Innercise*

"You won't be able to put *The Desire Factor* down! This is a must read for anyone wanting to create any desire no matter how big or small."

—Marci Shimoff, author of *Happy for No Reason*

"The quality of the life experience that each of us is now living in is the result of the quality of energy we've been offering. The formula for manifesting any type of internal or external change we desire is simple. Change the energy we're sending so it's in alignment with a different result."

—Brian Tracy, author of *Maximum Achievement*

"The only thing that stops any of us from living our best lives is the limitations we place upon ourselves. We desire abundance, happiness, and creative expression but hold doubts about our ability to attain those things. *The Desire Factor* expertly guides you through a seven-step process for releasing the brakes you're unconsciously placing on yourself, so you have the freedom to generate energetic alignment with any outcome you desire to create."

—Mary Morrissey, founder of Brave Thinking Institute

"*The Desire Factor* is a must-read for anyone who wants to turn their intentions and desires into glorious Technicolor reality. The process that Christy Whitman outlines in *The Desire Factor* will show you how to align yourself on every level with your highest vision. This is the perfect handbook for our challenging times!"

—Colette Baron-Reid, Oracle expert and author of *The Map*

"*The Desire Factor* guides you sequentially through seven universal principles that will teach you how to align the energy of your thoughts, moods, beliefs, and expectations with whatever outcome you desire to manifest."

—John Gray, author of *Men Are from Mars, Women Are from Venus*

"*The Desire Factor* is a jewel that you will treasure for years to come. Rich with truth, this book is a guide that will help you get anything you seriously want. Wallace D. Wattles said, 'Desire is the unexpressed possibility within seeking expression without through our actions.' Desire is the yeast that raises the dough; it's the fuel that puts you on the right vibration to attract what you want in your life. Without it, you won't do what you have to do to be who you have to be to get what you really want. Christy has laid it out beautifully for you to read, enjoy, digest, and take action."

—Bob Proctor, bestselling author of *You Were Born Rich*

"In *The Desire Factor*, Christy Whitman shows readers precisely how to change your energy to create your desires, and presents this information in bite-size steps—seven, to be exact. The book is also rich with interactive processes that afford readers a firsthand experience of what it feels like to effect a shift in their energy, and to realize the profound external changes that come about as a result."

—Sonia Choquette, *New York Times* bestselling author of *Trust Your Vibes*

"Christy and The Council are delivering what the world needs right now. The new and original wisdom found in *The Desire Factor* is the perfect and important blend of universal wisdom and practical how-to steps to face your fears, fulfill your desires, and find yourself creating the life that you finally love. You are about to be proud of the life you are creating and sense true fulfillment. The Council is one of the best places to turn for the most relevant and current insights. This book delivers, get this right now!"

—Jennifer McLean, creator of the Global Phenomenon:
The Spontaneous Tranformation Technique

"*The Desire Factor* is a phenomenal guide on how to consciously connect and create the life you desire. Like a tuning fork for a musician, this book inspires the reader to resonate and align with their highest good."

—Neil Giraldo, musician, producer, and songwriter

"We all have desires, all the time . . . large, small, expected, inexplicable, and everything in between. Christy Whitman's *The Desire Factor* brilliantly dives deep into the core of what's behind our 'silly dreams,' revealing that indeed the longings of our soul are signals from God, Universe's beacons for our path. Her methodology takes the guilt and shame out of the equation and goes all the way to the why, all while cleverly tackling some heavy philosophical topics with humor, wit, and charm. I can't recommend this book enough!"

—Anna Trebunskaya, professional dancer on *Dancing with the Stars*

"*The Desire Factor* is a much-needed guide to help you pursue what truly inspires you at work."

—Ashley Stahl, career coach, speaker, and author of *You Turn*

"*The Desire Factor* is a simple, straightforward guide for harnessing the powerful, unseen forces that orchestrate every act of creation. This book is a must-read for anyone seeking to manifest any desire."

—Shanda Sumpter, queen visionary and CEO of HeartCore Business

"*The Desire Factor* is a must-read book if you want to be a deliberate creator in your life. No matter how big or small your desires may be this book is the tool to help your desires become a reality."

—Sheila Gillette, channel for THEO

"Passion is an important aspect in creating your desires. Energy is the source of all manifested things, and *The Desire Factor* is the definitive guide to achieving energy mastery. This is a must-read for anyone that has any desire, big or small!"

—Janet Bray Attwood, *New York Times* bestselling author of *The Passion Test*

"*The Desire Factor* uncovers a simple and profound formula for aligning with the frequencies of consistent abundance and fulfillment, regardless of the desire you have. Feeling an internal connection, all your greatest desires unfold easily and swiftly."

—Anita Moorjani, *New York Times* bestselling author of *Dying to Be Me* and *What If This Is Heaven?*

"Christy Whitman takes the mystery out of manifestation with this beautifully written, clear, and insightful guide on how to create all that your heart desires. Her optimistic encouragement will inspire you to go for the gold in life. A must-read for those on the path of personal empowerment and collective awakening."

—Katherine Woodward Thomas, *New York Times* bestselling author of *Calling in "The One"*

"One of the seven principles to *The Desire Factor* is the Principle of Loving. Since love is the most powerful, creative energy in the universe, we must not only love ourselves, but love our desires as if we already have them. This book is a must-read for anyone wanting to release their fears and doubts and start living into their deepest desires."

—Dee Wallace, actress, author, and healer

"What a relief it is to find someone who doesn't chastise you for desiring that sleek new Tesla or decadent trip to the Greek Isles, but rather illuminates the intrinsic value of *all* desires. The knowledge and tools in *The Desire Factor* are fresh and unique. This is not a rehashing of what we already know but a completely new angle that can change the trajectory of your life forever."

—Debra Poneman, bestselling author and founder of Yes to Success seminars

The Desire Factor

How to Embrace Your Materialistic Nature
to Reclaim Your Full Spiritual Power

Christy Whitman

BEYOND WORDS
Portland, Oregon

BEYOND WORDS

1750 S.W. Skyline Blvd., Suite 20
Portland, OR 97221-2543
503-531-8700 / 503-531-8773 fax
www.beyondword.com

First Beyond Words paperback edition April 2021

Beyond Words Publishing is an imprint of Simon & Schuster, Inc., and the Beyond Words logo is a registered trademark of Beyond Words Publishing, Inc.
For information about special discounts for bulk purchases, please contact Beyond Words Special Sales at 503-531-8700 or specialsales@beyondword.com.

Managing editor: Lindsay S. Easterbrooks-Brown
Copyeditor: Ali Shaw
Proofreader: Olivia Rollins
Design: Sara E. Blum
Composition: William H. Brunson Typography Services

Manufactured in the United States of America

10 9 8 7 6 5 4 3 2 1

Library of Congress Cataloging-in-Publication Data

Names: Whitman, Christy, author.
Title: The desire factor : how to embrace your materialistic nature to
   reclaim your full spiritual power / Christy Whitman.
Description: Portland : Beyond Words, 2021. | Summary: "The Desire Factor
   proves that desire is the force behind every act of creation. It is the
   mechanism through which everything in this boundless spiritual universe
   is made manifest into physical, tangible form. The Desire Factor unfolds the
   precise steps for bringing about the manifestation of any desire. Take
   author Christy Whitman's advice and learn to lean in to prosperity and
   abundance"— Provided by publisher.
Identifiers: LCCN 2020029411 (print) | LCCN 2020029412 (ebook) |
   ISBN 9781582707594 (paperback) | ISBN 9781582707600 (ebook)
Subjects: LCSH: Desire. | Creative ability. | Personality. | Success.
Classification: LCC BF575.D4 W45 2021 (print) | LCC BF575.D4 (ebook) |
   DDC 153.3/5--dc23
LC record available at https://lccn.loc.gov/2020029411
LC ebook record available at https://lccn.loc.gov/2020029412

The corporate mission of Beyond Words Publishing, Inc.: *Inspire to Integrity*

To you, the reader, who called this information into being. As all things are in the universe, this was a cocreative project with you and me. Thank you.

To Frederic, Alex, and Max, for all the infinite love you give to me each and every day.

To the Council. I am so grateful and blessed. And I am so happy to have you serve through me.

To implement this information on a deeper level and receive all the processes and guided meditations, go to www.thedesirefactor.com/action

Contents

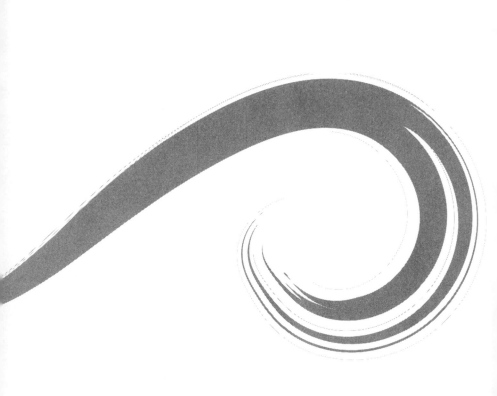

Foreword

The universal principles that bring about every act of creation are neither arbitrary nor difficult to understand. They work the same for everyone, regardless of age, status, color, or culture. Each of us is the center of all that we attract into our lives. What we align with—on the physical level of our bodies and surroundings as well as on the energetic level of our thoughts, perceptions, and attitudes—we draw to us.

My work as a feng shui master and as one of the master teachers in the global phenomenon *The Secret* is focused entirely around the principle of attraction. I have taught millions of people how to create success, abundance, positive relationships, well-being, and enlightenment by using the Law of Attraction in their physical environment. Your home and workspace are the physical vessel where you can receive the success, prosperity, and love that you desire to bring in. In this book, my friend and colleague Christy Whitman also shows you how to access this state of receptivity, not through altering your physical environment but through deliberately tuning the energy conduit that is your human mind-body apparatus.

I met Christy several years ago through the Transformational Leadership Council, of which I am a founding member. As we got to know one another better, I learned that Christy is a messenger for the Quantum Council, a collective consciousness of ascended masters here to teach others how to create all that they desire in the physical world through utilizing the spiritual laws of abundance. For over twenty-five years, Christy has been studying, practicing, and sharing with others the principles and techniques for mastering energy. This book is a distillation of that ever-evolving body of knowledge, and it takes readers from the basic understanding that thoughts create into a whole new level of fluency in the language of vibration.

The Desire Factor is organized according to seven universal principles—alignment, focus, joyful expectancy, having, loving, surrender, and action—each of which builds on the last. It's also rich with personal stories that demonstrate precisely how these principles are at work behind the scenes in the unfolding of all of our day-to-day experiences. As you understand these principles and gain skill and confidence at applying them, you will shift the quality and nature of all that you attract.

The personality that you think of as *you* is inextricably connected to the intelligence of the universe itself. You were born with an innate ability to align with this broader aspect of you and to receive a continual flow of all the insights and inspiration that will lead you to the realization of a joyous, satisfying life experience. This book will show you how to manifest all that you desire by living in that sublime state of flow.

—Marie Diamond
Feng Shui Master and Master Teacher in *The Secret*
www.mariediamond.com

INTRODUCTION

The Spiritual Nature of Material Desire

Desire. It's a powerful force that triggers a surge of heightened pleasure and purpose, sending life-giving energy rushing through every fiber of our beings. And regardless of whether the object of our desire is a person, a possession, or an idea that we want to make manifest in our lives, the act of wanting something is about far more than its attainment. Desire is a catalyst that can awaken our highest qualities, our greatest human potential, and our full spiritual power.

Like the proverbial carrot dangling from a stick that gives the mule a reason to keep striving toward a destination, the act of acknowledging a desire also leads us on a journey. And this is not only a journey toward simply *having* but also a journey of *becoming*. Desire is intended to feed you, to thrill and refresh you, and every desire, big or small, summons life force itself through you. And yet, each of us must make the choice to grant our desires permission to be, and to tend to any resistant or opposing thoughts that contradict them. When we surrender to this process by allowing our desires to blossom—first within the unseen realm of our own heart and mind, and ultimately in full manifestation in the three-dimensional world—they have the potential to guide us to our fullest spiritual expression and our most abundant life. I have had countless experiences of this throughout my life.

In my early twenties, I began what would become a lifelong love affair with high fashion and designer brands. Matching an adorable handbag with the perfect pair of shoes was for me an exalted—even spiritual—experience. I remember the exact day when, after being struck with what seemed to be a superficial attraction to a luxurious handbag, I was led upon a profound journey of becoming. I'd been browsing in a department store in downtown Chicago when I spotted, and instantly fell in love with, an adorable little saddlebag purse made by Coach. Now, in comparison to my salary at the time, the price tag was definitely a stretch—and most reasonable people would never have even considered it. But everything about this purse excited me, so instead of feeling angry about how much it cost, I allowed my senses to drink in every glorious detail. I admired the softness of the leather, the quality of the stitching, its intoxicating scent. I walked out of the boutique that day resolved that I would, in time, become the owner of that purse.

As I continued along my window-shopping spree, envisioning myself carrying my new bag happily from store to store, I reached into my current purse for a cigarette and was stopped in my tracks by a powerful insight: I had been a pack-a-day smoker for years, and while I knew it wasn't good for me, I had never found enough motivation to quit. I suddenly realized that the version of me who would one day carry that adorable Coach handbag would never dream of using it to hold a smelly pack of cigarettes! In that moment, I saw that I could use my desire to buy that purse as both the leverage and the reward to finally quit smoking, and sure enough, this desire—and the possibility contained within it—gave me all the incentive

I needed. My desire for that handbag was not nearly as superficial as it may have seemed. It was an agent that the Divine was using to guide me to my next level of health and vitality.

About fifteen years after this event, I experienced a similar calling. I was on vacation in Venice, Italy, with my mom and dad and my then-boyfriend Frederic, who is now my husband. As I walked through the beautiful cobblestone streets, I felt as if I'd stepped into a fashionista Shangri-La. Designer boutiques lined the streets as far as the eye could see: Chanel, Prada, Gucci, Versace, Dolce & Gabbana . . . oh my! As I stepped into the fifth or sixth store, my eyes locked on a stunning hand-stitched Fendi handbag, perfect in every way—with the single exception of the price tag, which happened to be three thousand dollars. At that time, nothing about spending three thousand dollars on a handbag would have been a good idea. I had just left my steady, fifteen-year career in corporate America to follow my passion of becoming a life coach, and my fledgling business was barely off the ground. I had to be mindful of every expense. Still, I really, really wanted that purse! To me, it represented elegance, abundance, and beauty—qualities that I very

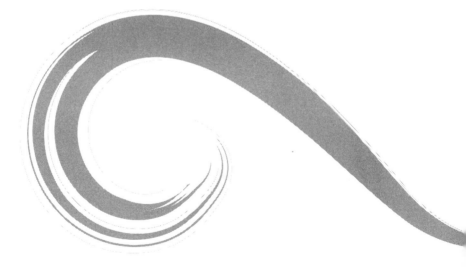

much wanted to include, nourish, and enhance in my experience. Without realizing it, in that moment of nonresisted desire, I set into motion another process of becoming. I told myself that I would return to Venice someday and purchase a purse of my choosing—a marker of and a reward for my success.

As I write these words today, having devoted the past twenty or more years to studying, applying, and teaching others about the powerful universal laws that govern the process of all manifestation, I now understand the full spiritual significance of the flashes of insight I received on each of those days.

Those coveted purses had been symbols that helped me focus my attention and creative energy toward much bigger and more important goals: The Coach bag symbolized my becoming a woman who is healthy, active, self-loving, energetic, and—naturally—a nonsmoker. And that, by the way, is the woman who returned to that very boutique two months later, cigarette-free, and walked out with a Coach purse on her arm. Similarly, the Fendi bag was a symbol of success; when I envisioned myself carrying it, I saw a woman who is confident and accomplished, who has the freedom to spend her money and time in ways that are pleasing to her and that contribute meaningfully to others.

The day I spotted the Coach purse, I was not only a pack-a-day smoker; I was also twenty pounds overweight. Discouraged after a string of bad relationships, I truly did not like myself very much. The day I saw the Fendi bag, my experience of life was one of having a shortage of both time and money. But nine years later, when I returned to Venice with my husband, two children, and my parents (a gift provided to my parents at Christmas), I declared I would purchase whatever purse most excited me regardless of the price. As I spent a wonderful day with Frederic going into every shop (he is such a good sport!), I saw *the one*. Walking into Dolce & Gabbana, I purchased the perfect symbol of my success. And I did so with the full pride and satisfaction of knowing that I had created a multimillion-dollar coaching business that not only serves others but also rewards me with an abundance of both time and money. My desire for each of these material objects provided the vehicle, the awareness, and the avenue to discover and manifest the next version of myself that the higher part of me was urging me to become.

Purses, for me, ignite the Desire Factor. They light me up, summon energy through me, and give me a glimpse into a new, yet-unrealized reality. This is the divine purpose of desire, whether the desire itself is for something material or something intangible; big or small. Designer bags and shoes may inspire zero interest for the next girl, but it's not about the items, the destination, or the specifics of any particular manifestation. It's about the process of being lit up by something and the energy that is summoned through you as a result. The particular objects that you desire—whether they are big or small, tangible or intangible—are of no consequence. The real value lies in discovering that you want something more, better, or different than what you currently have and then allowing this life-giving realization to stir something within you. When you make the decision to use your desires for this expansive and spiritual purpose, you are actively cooperating with the Desire Factor within you.

The word *desire*, by the way, is defined by Webster's dictionary as "a conscious impulse toward something that promises enjoyment or satisfaction in its attainment." And we experience this on every level of our being. From a purely physiological perspective, whenever we desire something, dopamine is released in our brain, triggering a surge of heightened pleasure, focus, and aliveness. From a spiritual perspective, the act of wanting something, and of aligning ourselves with the image of its fulfillment, is what enables us to see the next greatest version of ourselves that the larger part of us is calling us to become. When we understand desire from the perspective that it is a conscious impulse being transmitted to us from our Divine Self, from the nonphysical part of us, we can truly be fulfilled, expanded, and excited by it.

Desire is the first step in all creation. Without desire, nothing happens, and there can be no motion forward. Without desire, the universe and the planet on which we are all living would not have been created. Without desire, you would not exist. Burning desires come forth as an activity of your Divine Self, stirring you up to realize that it wants to do more for you, with you, and through you. You can be certain that when you want something—provided it's not hurtful to you or anyone else, and it will bring good into your life—it is your spiritual Divine Self tugging at your heart's door, trying to get your attention. When you accept the existence of that desire, you must then accept the fulfillment of it. You must decide that you want it and become an active participant in the having of it.

Desire is one way to bring the human and unconscious part of you into alignment with the larger part of you, your Divine Self. Every desire you have really is a divine desire. Every frustration you have in the attainment of the desire happens so that you can integrate your boundless higher self with your time-bound personality. Desiring the partner, the money, the house, the shoes, the car, the vacations . . . they are ideas arising from the Divine for the purpose of bringing you back home to yourself. Any area of your life where you're experiencing less than joy and fulfillment is a reflection that your creative potential is still asleep. And in an attempt to awaken you, your higher self gives you a burning desire. The burning desire at its core is a call for completeness, a call to return you home to yourself.

Contrary to what most of us have been socialized to believe, the desires that arise within us are neither good nor bad. A heartfelt desire to become a parent or meet the man or woman of your dreams is not inherently nobler than a desire to travel the world, make an impact in your career in service to others, or purchase a high-end purse. There is so much judgment cast upon people who openly express desire for material things, and this is the very epitome of irony, because—to paraphrase what pop icon Madonna noted all those years ago—we are *all* material boys and girls, living in a material world. Desire is not an evil agent intended to separate man from God's grace; it is the avenue by which we come to understand the divinity that we are and to enjoy the full bounty of the abundant universe in which we live.

From spiritual traditions and pop culture alike, most of us have been deeply ingrained with the message that the pursuit of desire is evil and hedonistic, and that spirituality and materialism cannot, and should not, coexist. The Bible cites desire as the reason that Adam and Eve—having been lured by Satan to eat from the Tree of Knowledge of Good and Evil—fell from God's grace and were cast out of the Garden of Eden. Hinduism and Buddhism tell us that in order to realize our full spiritual nature, we must renounce all desire for worldly things. And so, whether intentionally or unconsciously, most of us attempt to diminish the strength of our own wanting.

How many of us allow doubt and disbelief to suffocate our dreams before we ever give them a chance to bloom? How many try to kill our desires off by rationalizing, defending, and justifying them to others or to ourselves?

The programming that desire is the root of all suffering, or that material things are inherently bad, stems from a belief that we lack the ability to attain those things. We judge desire as bad because we doubt that we deserve to live the good life or have it all. But all of us are divinely designed to have the good life. We are all born to have it all and to experience what we would love in all aspects of our individual lives, connected to the very life that breathes us.

The desire to experience something new—whether it's a new purse, a new pair of shoes, a new house, or a new level of financial prosperity—is not shallow. These desires are born within us in order to lead us to realize and to then bring into existence more of our greatness, our potential, and our unique gifts.

As you will come to understand by the time you are finished reading this book, every desire that arises within us—whether it's for a tangible object or an intangible experience—is calling us forward in the way that those handbags called to me. We all have heartfelt desires that, if allowed to gather momentum rather than be suppressed by doubt or fear, will bring us more sharply into focus, summon us more deliberately into action, and inspire us to tap into more of our talents, wisdom, and latent resources. The focal points that capture our attention will naturally be different for each of us, however, because we are all seeking to grow, expand, and express ourselves in unique ways.

Recently, I was chatting with my friend Patty, who lights up every time she tells me about her desire to travel through Wyoming. Something about exploring the rugged, undeveloped landscape fills her with a sense of adventure that her soul has been yearning for. Wyoming is Patty's Desire Factor, and if she follows the path that this desire will lay out in front of her, it will lead her not only to Wyoming but also to the next evolution of the person she desires to be. It could even lead her to a life she can't even conceive of from where she stands right now.

Now, is there some special magic that can be found only in Wyoming? Absolutely not! Likewise, there was no inherent magic in the Coach handbag that I used to inspire myself to stop smoking—and later to lose twenty pounds, and to collect a closet full of gorgeous clothes—or in the Fendi purse that inspired me to create an abundant life. It's never about the thing; it's about who we become when we surrender to the desire to have it. Regardless of the specific objects of your desire, the pursuit of them is a spiritual one, because who you will become in the process of attaining them will serve as a catalyst for your own growth and evolution.

Every desire that pulses through your veins and every idea that occurs to you as a result of this does so because the spiritual energy that sources you at your very core and connects you to All

That Is—whether you call it God, Goddess, Spirit, Source, or the Creator—is seeking to experience and express itself through your body, your senses, your mind, and your perspective. You might commune with this nonphysical counterpart silently or aloud, or you may have assigned it a particular name or form. But what's vital to understand is that your relationship with your Divine Self is ongoing and ever evolving. The strength of your connection may ebb and flow at different times throughout your life, and your experience of it may also change over time.

Earlier in my life, I experienced my connection with source energy as a silent presence that communicated with me mainly through intuition and downloads of insight that guided me in the direction of my highest good. Now, its messages come through in distinct blocks of thought, offered to me by a collection of nonphysical ascended masters that call themselves the Quantum Council. As you'll soon discover, the Council has a unique way of saying things, and—because they are entirely nonphysically focused—they offer a perspective that is often very different from my own. To give you a direct experience of the depth of their wisdom, I've included direct quotes offered by the Council at the beginning of each chapter.

The Council's intention is to help humanity embrace our innate creative power and to understand that we are divinely designed to experience well-being, abundance, success, and loving relationships. As someone who has been intentionally tuning to higher levels of consciousness for more than half my life, I am able to receive these energetic transmissions and find language to translate their messages into words, but this kind of communion is available to all who deliberately attend to strengthening their connection.

Each of us receives these impulses from our creator in our own unique way, and each of us in turn provides for our creator a unique avenue through which this energy can flow and express itself through our human attributes. We are not separate from the nonphysical source that created us and all things—we are an insep-arable, integrated part of it. But, by the power of our own free will, we can choose to hold ourselves temporarily apart from the energy of our creator by virtue of the thoughts we think and the perceptions we hold to be true.

When we perceive ourselves as separate from the nonphysical source that created all things; when we mistakenly believe that the three-dimensional material world is all that exists; when we allow ourselves to believe that there are evil forces with the power to insert themselves into our experience; when we become so addicted to drama, chaos, conflict, and struggle that we actu-ally come to think of these conditions *as* ourselves, we cut ourselves off—albeit temporarily—from the innermost part of ourselves that is one with our cre-ator. As a result of the limitations of our own thinking, we feel horrible, we feel disjointed, our desires torture us rather than thrill us, and what manifests around us in the outer world of form reflects our state of internal disconnection.

The awareness that our present reality is not everything we would like it to be is what gives birth to the very first seed of desire. This desire—whether for improvement, for greater comfort, or for something entirely different than what we have—is always inspired by the creator, and to ignore, deny, suppress, or judge this inspiration is to cut ourselves off from the very source of our spiritual sustenance. But when a desire is born within us and we nourish it with positive thoughts and beliefs, when we allow ourselves to fall in love with the very idea of its unfolding, and when we celebrate and appreciate the manifestation of what we want wherever and in whomever we see it, that desire provides a vehicle through which we can realize everything that we have the potential to become.

Maybe you are—like I have been all these years—inspired by shiny things. Maybe you'd love to create a customized, handmade wardrobe or have a walk-in closet filled with designer shoes. Maybe it's a particular experience you're seeking, in the same way my friend Patty craves the experience of traveling through Wyoming. A couple of years back, the factor that inspired my son Alex to new levels of discipline and focus was his desire to earn his yellow belt in karate. And by the time you are reading these words, Alex will have undoubtedly hatched many more desires to use as his focal point for the expansion he seeks.

Each of the spiritual principles I'll be guiding you through in this book—including the Principle of Alignment, the Principle of Focus, the Principle of Joyful Expectancy, the Principle of Having, the Principle of Loving, the Principle of Surrender, and the Principle of Action—will begin to overwrite the messages that most of us received early on that conditioned us to repress and deny our desires. Statements such as *Money doesn't grow on trees*, *The world does not revolve around you*, or *You can't always get what you want* convinced us early on that resources in this universe are scarce and therefore a successful life must be focused on compromise rather than seeking fulfillment. But as we'll explore in great detail in the next chapter, the universe in which we live is not limited in any way but is designed to expand to accommodate virtually every desire that we allow to be born within us.

It is my hope to help you become aware, understand, and know that the experiences you truly desire in life, whatever they may be, will not come to you through settling, compromising, or striving to keep yourself small. Desires are not birthed to make you worry, disappoint you, or frustrate you. If you desire something that you feel you can't have, then you are holding yourself apart from your spiritual power. You have what I call "split energy" about a desire: wanting it but not believing you can have it. The full satisfaction and exaltation you seek will begin to unfold as you allow the full force of your desires to move you in the direction of your expansion. It is this expansion that you really want, and repressing it is simply not an option.

Through your connection with the Divine, your energy partner, you have the ability to bring about any change you wish to realize in your life. You have the power within you at this very moment to realize the fulfillment of your every desire.

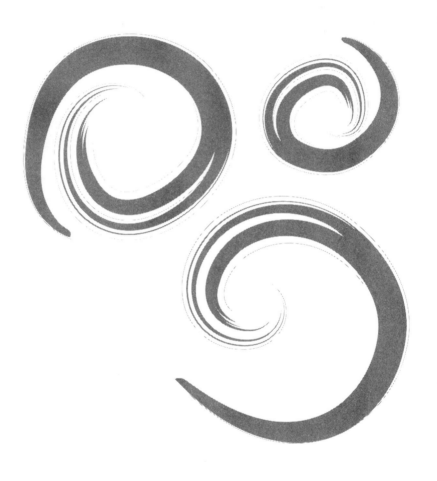

1

The Principle of Alignment

Alignment is the key to everything you desire. If you are not connected to the power source from which the desire came, you are out there trying, willing, and forcing your desires into form. You are divinely designed to thrive and feel good, and that means your desires are an extension of that alignment to your source.

The Quantum Council

How is it that desires are made manifest? How come some people seem to manifest so easily with great results while others struggle for years—if not their entire lifetimes—trying to create what they want? What exactly is the formula for becoming the happy, abundant, wildly successful versions of ourselves that we truly wish to be? And how is it that our thoughts—seemingly so etheric and intangible—turn into objective, material realities like relationships, cars, career breakthroughs, magnificent vacations, and high-end handbags?

1

It may seem that taking physical, concrete action is the obvious—even the only—path to creating all of the above. And the more we intensely desire something, or the bigger that desire looms in the distance, then the greater the effort we feel we need to apply. This is the essence of the *no pain, no gain* mind-set that so many are still living within, which tells us that paying our dues and working hard is the only way to fulfill our hearts' desires. Clearly, we can accomplish certain things just by applying physical force and mental effort. After all, just about everyone is capable of devising a plan and executing it, in the same way we can move a pile of rocks from one place to another.

But what about the fulfillment of truly extraordinary—even miraculous—desires? Is physical action alone responsible for the sudden flash of insight that evolves into a multimillion-dollar enterprise? Is mental effort the principal force at work within the artist who writes a song in fifteen minutes that wins her a Grammy and becomes a part of pop culture forevermore? What about the "chance" meeting that delivers you face-to-face with your soul mate, or the single piece of information that drops into your lap and ushers in a whole new way of life?

These are all examples of big accomplishments that seem to manifest easily—even out of the blue—and of course, those experiences are thrilling. But what about those small, everyday desires that sometimes manifest spontaneously and effortlessly? A few years ago, my husband, Frederic, and I had only just begun to softly ponder the idea of selling our house. Really, we'd barely even spoken about it. Five days later, through a completely effortless and mind-blowing sequence of events, our house sold for the exact amount we wanted to receive, without us ever listing it on the market or even taking a single photo. A textbook definition of the spontaneous manifestation of desire.

Could planning, strategizing, or forcing the issue have yielded us the same result? Maybe. But trying to manifest your desires the hard way through willpower and force is not what this book is about. The outcome that Frederic and I created—just like the outcomes created by the thousands of people I've coached through the years—was the result of our *alignment*. In those moments in time when our hearts and minds are in perfect sync with our divine nature, we are at our most creative and resourceful. Our actions are inspired rather than contrived, and they are far more effective because they are backed up and sourced by our full spiritual power. There is an unobstructed flow between the physical and nonphysical aspects of us, and this connection yields far greater results than anything we can accomplish from a disconnected state. This is the power of the Principle of Alignment.

When a desire—big or small—manifests this easily, it feels almost miraculous. But it's not a miracle. The people in this world who are the happiest; who have energy, vitality, and clarity; who have plenty of money, creative self-expression, and loving and supportive relationships aren't accomplishing these things through hard work or effort alone. They are allowing them into their experience through their alignment. And the manifestations themselves are rarely the primary source—and certainly not a lasting source—of their happiness. The real joy comes from the feeling of being in the flow of life and having the direct experience that the universe is our willing, cooperative, creative partner.

Whether it's the manifestation of a ten-million-dollar winning lottery ticket or the manifestation of a choice parking spot at the mall at Christmastime, the joy and satisfaction we feel as we watch something we desire fall into place comes from knowing that we attracted that outcome to us, through our clarity, our receptivity, and our alignment. We allowed ourselves to be guided to the right place at the right time, and we accurately interpreted the clues that were being offered to us by the benevolent universe of which we are all important parts.

In truth, these clues—which have the very real potential of leading us quickly and joyfully to the spontaneous realization of everything we desire—are all around us, all the time, pointing the way toward everything we desire in every important aspect of our lives. But to pick up on them with clarity and accuracy, we have to be open to receive. In other words, the energy we are broadcasting through our thoughts, our moods, and—importantly—our expectations must be in energetic resonance with the outcome we desire.

It's All about Energy

We now know that everything within this seemingly material universe, ourselves included, is made up of energy. Einstein proved this, and modern science and quantum physics have further confirmed and expanded on the understanding. What appears to our senses as solid matter is simply energy, vibrating at different rates of speed. Your eyes translate light waves into sight. Your ears translate sound waves into hearing. But nothing material actually exists. And this means that the "stuff" that makes up the entire universe is actually not stuff at all. It's energy.

Energy is the currency of life. It's the force that animates all things. When it's flowing through you with the inhalation and exhalation of each breath, the doctors proclaim you to be alive. And when the energy that creates all things stops flowing through you, they pronounce you dead. Now, I am not a doctor or a scientist or a physicist. I don't get especially geeked out on taking things apart in order to find out what makes them tick. I send and receive texts and emails all the time without understanding exactly how that delivery takes place, and I'm quite content to flip a light switch without learning the ins and outs of electricity. My approach to manifestation is an energetic and spiritual one, which has been tried and tested in my own experience and in the experiences of my students and clients. But if you desire a more scientific understanding of the energetic nature of the universe, know that there are plenty of books out there that explain these concepts brilliantly.

I am a teacher of energy mastery, which is simply the practice of deliberately aligning one's personal energy field with the energy stream that creates and sources all things. We are each extensions of this nonphysical energy and are inextricably and unendingly connected to it. You may not be consciously aware of this connection, but your alignment with your source is at the basis of every exalted or inspired moment. Whether you refer to this energy as Life Force, Infinite Intelligence, Mother Nature, Source, Spirit, Soul, or God makes no difference whatsoever. This broader energy is the essence of who you are. It is the very source of you. It's the force that breathes you, that gives you life and sustains you through this lifetime and beyond. It's the boundless supply of everything you could possibly need or desire. Although you were born in a physical body, which uses physical senses to perceive, the vast majority of you remains as this nonphysical, divine energy. This is the same presence and power through which the entire universe was created. And it is your life partner—your energy partner—along this journey.

Right now as you read these words, you could say there are two of you having this experience. There is an outer you and an inner you; an earth-bound self that will live and die, and a Divine Self that can never be bound by the limitations of earth life. This part of you actually functions on a deeper level, on a higher energy vibration. And you have access to its power always.

This benevolent energy stream, which I will refer to as your Divine Self throughout this book, wants you to be radiantly healthy, because health is its perfect expression. It wants you to be prosperous, because abundance is its very nature. It wants you to be happy, to feel perfectly at peace, loving and loved, wise, successful, confident, enthusiastic, joyful, strong, and free, because these states of being reflect its wholeness, completeness, and perfect harmony and because *you* are an extension of this. Within this energy field is everything that we could ever possibly desire, not only for this current life but also for all of eternity.

You are a spiritual being living in a physical world. You are an extension of the source that created all things. Most of your being—what you might label your spirit, your consciousness, or your soul—remains in that higher, infinite dimension while your mental, emotional, and physical bodies are focused in the third dimension of time and space. Your objective here—your life purpose, so to speak—is to enjoy the physical plane experience without losing sight of your true identity in the fog of materiality. You are here to live, love, laugh, and happily manifest all of your desires without the emotional bondage of fear, guilt, greed, or sorrow.

Your role in this world is to have everything without possessing anything—to enjoy an abundance of wealth without being preoccupied with making money, to have right livelihood without struggling to make a living, to have wholeness without focusing on the body, to have right relations without selfish emotional affections. You have the power within you at this very moment to realize the fulfillment of every desire. Through the love, wisdom, and power of your Divine Self, your inner being, your life partner, you have the ability to shift any circumstance, situation, relationship—*everything*—right now. And this mastery begins with an acknowledgment of the powerful, vibrational being that you are.

The divine, universal energy that sources you is ever-present to assist you in the manifestation of all that you desire. It is always available to you; always at your back. This energy is at the basis of everything, and there is no beginning, ending, or limit to this potent, powerful source energy. And here, of course, the questions naturally arise: If the energy that creates all things exists in abundant supply and is equally available to everyone, then why is it that some people manifest their desires so fluidly and naturally while others are living lives of struggle, mediocrity, or quiet desperation? If divine energy is at the basis of all things and we all have equal access to it, then how is it that some people are using it to create their version of heaven on earth while others—by depriving themselves of it—are creating a living hell? What are the hidden mechanics behind the reality that each of us is living, and why is that reality so vastly different for each of us?

The answer to all of these questions is the same. Everything comes down to the alignment, or misalignment, of our own personal energy field. The energy that creates worlds is available to each of us at all times, but as individuals, we have the option of allowing it to fuel us, inspire us, and guide us, and we also have the option of remaining ignorant of its astounding power and therefore denying ourselves access to it. This is the incredible power of free will. The degree of our happiness or unhappiness, our satisfaction or deprivation, and our experience of abundance or lack is simply a reflection of our relationship with this energy stream. And that relationship is entirely within our control.

The universe is always cooperating with us. To the extent that our personal energy is aligned with that which we desire, our desires manifest easily. And to the extent that we are out of alignment—whether in thought, belief, mood, or expectation—we continue to hold the outcomes we want at arm's length. Whether we create a joyful, abundant life or a life of struggle and hardship is a direct result of how we perceive the world and how we perceive ourselves in relationship to it.

Spirits in a Material World

Because you—a nonphysical, all-powerful, divine being—were born into a physical world that's filled with other people, structures, and conditions that are all perceivable through your five senses, it's easy to think of yourself as only a physical, flesh-blood-and-bone being living in a purely physical, material reality. It's easy to look around at people who have the things you want and decide that they must possess some special talent or advantage that you don't have, or that they were born with a "lucky horseshoe up their butt"—a charming expression that was used in my household when I was growing up.

It's easy to conclude that life is unfair or random and that there is no real rhyme or reason behind the huge disparity in the levels of well-being, prosperity, and joy that some are living in comparison to the rest. It's actually very common to believe that it's not possible to have it all, so even if we do manage to scrape together some success in one area of life—such as in relation to our finances or career expression—we'll have to pay for it by sacrificing in other areas, such as our physical well-being or the quality of our intimate relationships. And as we believe, so we create.

As we look around at the world in which we all live, it's easy to conclude that there is one objective reality that each of us interacts with in the same way. And by an objective reality, I mean something that exists independently of the consciousness that perceives it. But the fact is—and hold on to your hat here—nothing objective exists. Everything is subjective, meaning that the experiences we call "reality" are created, by

8

each of us, through the power of our perception. I know this might sound pretty far out there, so let's ground it by considering a couple of simplistic examples.

When you look at a tree and conclude that its leaves are green, is that because there is an actual green substance flowing from the tree into your eyes? No. The experience you describe as green is nothing more than a frequency of energy that your senses interpret. "Green" doesn't exist anywhere in the world; it is created in consciousness, as all so-called material things are. Likewise, if you pass by a flower and decide that it's beautiful, does the beauty you saw exist within the flower? Or is it really true that beauty—along with ugliness, and everything else it's possible to experience—is in the eye of the beholder?

We are all deeply conditioned to perceive life as something that happens to us—independent of our perceptions, expectations, and emotions—when all along, life is happening from us. Action certainly plays a role in what does and does not manifest in our lives, but attention is the force that summons energy, and energy is the driving force behind every act of creation.

As you're about to learn in the section that follows, we are the creators of our own lives. We are the ones who interact with the energetic field from whence all things come and draw from its unbounded potential the precise components that will eventually culminate into the tangible manifestations of our lives.

Thanks to the truly mind-boggling discoveries in the field of quantum physics, we now understand that the universe is *not* a giant machine that unfolds predictably like the gears of a clock but is instead a highly intelligent, highly responsive field of energy and information that holds infinite possibilities. What we call "reality" is nothing but a blank canvas, and the pictures that each of us paints on that canvas are simply a reflection of our moment-to-moment internal state.

From Whence All Things Came

Picture this divine energy field that underlies, creates, and sustains all things, and imagine it as a light being filtered into an old-fashioned slide projector . . . well, into almost eight billion individual slide projectors, actually, at the time of this writing. As the light enters the machine and passes through each slide, an exact representation of that slide is magnified and projected on a screen or wall. The machine simply reflects the light, regardless of the image that's been placed inside. This is its job: to illumine, enliven, and make "real" whatever thought forms we can conceive.

In a similar way, the energy source that creates all things is like a light that is being projected to and through each of us, at all times, and in real time. And the images that are being displayed outward are simply projections of the consciousness of each of us at that moment. The universe provides the light, so to speak, that illumines whatever state of being we are generating within our individual consciousness. In simple terms, our thoughts, expectations, moods, and beliefs determine the realities that we create and then later observe. And, because no two observers hold the same intentions or expectations, no two realities are the same.

The unique energetic frequency of each individual interacts with the energy and information that make up the universe at large. As part of this interaction, the individual's energetic frequency manifests this information into the particular objects, experiences, and outcomes that become that individual's life experience. There is no one objective world that everyone perceives collectively. Instead, the universe really is, as Deepak Chopra writes in his bestselling book *The Seven Spiritual Laws of Success*, a "quantum soup" which each of us has an individual and deeply personal relationship with. We are the ones who assemble this quantum soup into our unique expression of reality. We are the ones who bring our own, in-the-moment frequency of energy to every situation and every relationship, and what we bring to the party energetically is exactly what we experience once we get there.

So think about it. You bring the potent energy of your thoughts, moods, and expectations into every situation you encounter. This means you were not a blank slate when you walked into that job interview, or when you went to meet that guy for a first date. In every interaction, the energy you walk in creates a trajectory for the experience you'll have when you walk out.

From an energetic perspective, the universe at large is like a giant, still pond. When we give our attention to a particular outcome—whether it's an outcome we want or don't want—it's like throwing a pebble into the center of that still pond. And the ripples that come back to the shore are what play out in real time as our life experiences. You are as continuous and interconnected with the universe as a wave is continuous and interconnected with the ocean. You are an integral part of the entire universe, and All That Is is responding to you. Allow that to settle in for a moment.

Take a deep breath. That breath is your Divine Self, breathing you. In truth, there is no separation between your human self and the infinite energy stream that sources you.

Our universe is an infinite energetic field that is swirling with every possibility. And because you, too, are an energetic being, you also hold the power to express yourself in infinite ways. The vibrations of your thoughts, moods, and expectations all generate a current, and just like the wind can turn the tide, you can energetically attract to yourself whatever experiences you desire.

Through the power of our observation, we call to us the energetic components that solidify, eventually, into the unique conditions of our lives. In other words, how you interact with the quantum field from whence all things come—and the expectations that you hold as you do—is what determines the reality that you create.

In your every waking moment, you are sending out an energetic or vibrational signal that is transmitted to the farthest corners of the universe. Your thoughts broadcast an energetic vibration, as do your emotions, your current and chronic moods, your dominant beliefs, and your moment-to-moment expectations. And this energy moves in currents and streams that are always leading in a particular direction. These waves of energy interact with the energy field of the universe at large, transforming the formless field of its quantum soup into flesh, blood, matter, and form. The manifestation of everything—from a high-end handbag to a galaxy—is orchestrated by this very process of attraction. Attraction is the mechanism that summons the energy that turns thoughts into things.

The Powerful, Universal Law of Attraction

Everything that manifests in the physical world does so by a process of resonant energies being drawn together. This is due to the phenomenon known as the Law of Attraction, which states that whatever energy we broadcast out into the universe is joined by and gathers to itself energies that are harmonic or resonant in frequency. Whatever we direct our powerful focus upon within the invisible realm of our thoughts, beliefs, and emotions eventually manifests into outer form. This means that the state of everything in our external world— our bodies, our relationships, the robustness of our careers and our finances—is a direct reflection of our internal state. In the simplest terms, the Law of Attraction is merely the principle that like attracts like. This law is universal, meaning it works for everyone, all the time, whether we are aware of it or not.

The Law of Attraction is neutral, in the same way that forces like gravity and electricity are neutral. They are absolutely consistent.

Electricity does not discriminate. It simply flows in response to the demand. You flip the switch on one of your appliances, and electricity is summoned to power it—whether it's a curling iron or a power saw. Likewise, the Law of Attraction summons the latent, powerful energy that creates everything in this universe and brings it to you, in direct response to your asking.

And while you do of course ask with your actions and your words, it is the energy behind your request that the universe is responding to. You ask with your vibration, which is to say the sum total of your most dominant perspectives, moods, attitudes, or beliefs in any given moment. The Principle of Alignment states that whatever experience or outcome you are energetically aligned with is the one you will create. In precise response to the vibration you're offering, the Law of Attraction gathers energies, experiences, people, and circumstances that match the vibration you are offering and delivers them directly, precisely, and unerringly to you.

This means that prior to every manifestation that we can see, hear, touch, or validate with any of our physical senses, there has been a tremendous movement of energetic components flowing in the direction of that eventual manifestation. Like the bulk of an iceberg, most of what is right this minute in the process of manifesting is completely invisible to us, and yet it is still gaining momentum as it is making its way into our experience. You become an energy master by making a concerted effort to perceive these unseen forces with the supremely sophisticated vibrational senses we were all born with and then by using your power of focus to harness them. Creation is nothing more than the activation of a vibration in advance of manifestation. And the reality you experience is entirely dependent on the vibration you are sending out.

The Radio Transmitter That Is You

A helpful way to understand this universal stream of energy that flows to and through all things is to think of it like the invisible radio signals that are constantly being transmitted through our airwaves. There are an infinite number of radio signals that are potentially accessible to each of us in every moment, but which of these we are actually able to receive depends entirely on the station our receivers are tuned to. So, what you hear—and see and taste, and smell and touch—in every aspect of your life is playing out that way in response to where and how you're setting your receiver. And here, my friends, is where free will and deliberate creation intersect in a very powerful way.

Most of the world does not know that they are the ones who set their dial. They don't realize that whatever is coming into their experience is coming in direct response to the way they are focusing their attention. Most have no clue about the power of thought, and so they make the critical mistake of permitting their vibration to be influenced by whatever is going on around them rather than offering their vibration on purpose. And as a result, they give all of their creative power over to external circumstances and other people, over which they have absolutely no control.

Let's go back to our radio example so you can get a better sense of what I mean. I'd like you to imagine that in the same way that your radio dial can tune in to a wide range of programs, the power of your focus can deliver you an even wider range of experiences. High-flying, good-feeling frequencies like inspiration, clarity, love, appreciation, and lightheartedness are at one end of the spectrum, and bad-feeling frequencies like powerlessness, despair, regret, and frustration exist at the low, slow, resistant end of the spectrum—in the same way there is a huge variety of radio stations along your radio dial. But if you're a person who has not yet learned that you can offer your vibration—and therefore create your experience of reality—independently of anything that is going on around you, you might allow your vibration to be influenced by the chaos of the world. This is, in fact, how most of the world is living. Something happens, they react, and then they blame that situation, or the person involved, for the way they feel.

So, for example, if you hit traffic while running late for a meeting, you naturally have more immediate access to the Frustration channel than you do the Blissfully Happy channel. If your partner breaks a date or you perceive her as ignoring you over dinner, you could definitely make the choice to tune in to the Bummed Out or Poor Me channels. If a project you care deeply about does not live up to your expectations when it rolls out, the Self-Criticism channel is right there, instantly accessible and blaring like a '90s boom box in your experience. And if self-criticism has been a vibration of choice for you, you most likely have that station on your presets! Of course, the Satisfaction channel is still broadcasting loud and clear on its own frequency, but from where your attention is focused, it's harder to find it. This is because the vibration you're tuned to exists within a particular spectrum of frequencies, and you can't pick up on anything that is outside your range. The energy of success carries a different vibration than that of failure. The energy of abundance moves at a different rate of speed than that of deprivation. And fear carries a drastically different frequency than love.

But here's the thing. You're still the one with your hand on the dial! You're still the one with the power to choose where you place your attention. All those other, good-feeling frequencies are still available. You could choose to focus on the Faith and Trust channel or to tune in to the sweet, soothing sounds of I'm Doing the Best I Can. Throughout this book, I'll show you many ways to master your energy in order to make this critical internal shift. For now, I just want you to be aware that you have this choice. You are always

15

the one who is in control of your reactions and, therefore, in control of your point of attraction. Exercising this muscle of internally controlling your own vibration by being deliberate about where you place your attention is essential to the process of manifesting anything you desire. Alignment is a moment-by-moment decision.

Whatever the reality you desire to bring into your life experience, it's nothing more than one probability that exists, like a radio station, within an infinite number of probabilities. And the way you attract it, invite it, and rendezvous with that reality above all others is by aligning your frequency with the frequency of that outcome. Using our radio example, if what you desire is broadcasting on 101.5 FM but your reaction to someone else's behavior has you circling the drain down at 98.6, that means there's a big disconnect between what you want and what you're attracting right now. This is called creation by default, and it's an extremely unpleasant, disempowering, unsatisfying way to live. We are energy receivers and are constantly receiving energy—whether from other people, from the experiences we're involved in, or from our Divine Self. Where our vibration is set determines what we receive.

Understanding Your Vibrational Range

So you get it, right? The energy you send out is magnetic, and just as a magnet attracts certain metal-based objects that are within its reach, you attract only the specific range of people, experiences, and outcomes that are vibrating within your current emotional range. You attract from the universe at large those particles of energy that are vibrating on a similar wavelength. And the frequency of the energy you habitually broadcast determines the frequency, or the quality, of the energy that comes back to you. If you look around your life experience and you are aware of manifestations that aren't to your liking, this means only one thing: you have been using your incredible powers of observation and attention in opposition to, rather than in alignment with, your Desire Factor.

So what determines whether you're living a life crippled by fear or a life accentuated with the most lavish abundance? It has everything to do with your utilization of the Principle of Alignment. You, as the observer of your unique life experience, summon into being the particles that come into your vibrational sphere, and thus you are the sole creator of that reality. Like a conductor of the most diverse and intricate orchestra, through the power of your attention, you create the symphony that becomes your life. From the vastness of the universe, you call into being a full, three-dimensional life experience. And the only difference between a life that sings with clarity and one that is filled with chaos and cacophony is the density of the vibrational tone that is being offered and responded to. That's it.

There is no limit to the amount of happiness we can experience. There is no limit to how much love, laughter, excitement, or satisfaction we can feel. This universe is unendingly abundant, which means that it has the ability to yield to us whatever experiences we desire. All we need to do to claim the abundance that is our birthright is to align ourselves with the energy of our own desires. Energy follows focus, and our emotions reflect the variation in our energy.

Once you accept that you are creating your life through the things you give your attention to, you will become much more intentional about how you apply that power. You'll realize that you simply can't afford to consider everything in this vast world, because doing so diffuses your creative power and scrambles your broadcast signal. So instead, you'll become as picky about what you give your attention to as you are about what you put in your mouth. And you'll come to appreciate and value highly one of the most important tools of a deliberate creator: focus.

Chapter 1: The Principle of Alignment— Applying It Step by Step

---

1   What is your Desire Factor? In some key aspect of your life, what is something that you currently want to manifest? It could be a condition, such as landing a better job. It could be a tangible object, such as a new or newer car. Or it could be something immaterial, such as a better-feeling relationship or greater health and vitality. Once you've identified what you want, speak it to yourself, either silently or out loud, as a statement of intent. "My Desire Factor is _____."

2   Next, consider why it is you want to manifest this particular desire. What about this desire inspires you or lights you up? What do you believe you will have access to by having it? For example, will you experience greater freedom? A sense of security or empowerment? Greater control over your own experience?

3 As you contemplate the fulfillment of your desire, how do you believe you will feel once you've attained it? Will you feel joyful? Lovable? Worthy? Secure? Acknowledge that the underlying reason that drives every desire is the belief that fulfilling it will cause us to feel a particular way. The more specifically you identify the underlying feeling you are actually reaching for, the more creative power you gain access to.

4 Acknowledge that this feeling essence of your desire exists, right now in this moment, as a particular energetic frequency that you have the ability to connect with and attune to. Establish and sustain this connection; the following exercise will support you.

Energy Mastery Exercise

Achieving Energetic Alignment
with the Essence of Your Desire

Begin this exercise by sitting comfortably on the floor or on a chair and gently closing your eyes. Take several deep breaths in and out to relax your body and clear your mind. Let go of any pressing thoughts or concerns, and allow yourself to settle into this moment, exactly as it is.

As you continue to breathe deeply, notice that your breath is actually a vehicle that connects your physical body with your energy body—the broader, nonphysical awareness that creates and sustains all things. Notice that placing your gentle awareness on your breath naturally begins to take you to the more subtle dimensions of your being . . . to the source or wellspring of all physical manifestations.

And with your next breath, gently bring into mind your Desire Factor. What is something you really want to manifest into your life right now? Take a moment to imagine this desired outcome or result, to see it as being a current part of your experience. Allow yourself to envision how the presence of this object, condition, or experience will shift your state of being. What will you gain greater access to by having this desire? Breathe this in, allowing the vibrational essence of your desire to penetrate your very being. Open yourself to the energy of it.

Deliberately breathe in the energetic essence of how you want to feel, and on your outbreath, release any energy you do not want. For example, if you want to feel peace, breathe in ease and flow, and breathe out tension. Breathe in light, and breathe out all negative energy or resistance.

Allow all aspects of your being—your body, your breath, your thoughts and feelings—to begin to sense the presence of the Divine flowing all around you and within you. Contemplate this body of light, this all-knowing, all-supportive, all-providing divine source of infinite love that is flowing through you always. Allow this joyful energy to fill your consciousness, and feel the dynamic power as your thoughts and emotions begin to pulsate in harmony with this higher, spiritual vibration. As you are now consciously aware of your Divine Self, imagine this infinite source of abundance and wisdom speaking these words to you:

> I am always here with you. I am your constant support, supply, and source, and all you need to do is ask and then allow yourself to receive. You are an individualized

expression of me; we are part of the same infinite energy stream. All that I am, you are also, because you are my physical counterpart—the most manifested expression of All That Is.

I am all that you can conceive of me to be. I am the source of your well-being, abundance, success, and loving and supportive relationships. Look to me as your all-sufficiency, knowing that nothing is ever withheld from you. And now, deliberately choose that which you desire, knowing that it is your divine inheritance and you are infinitely deserving of having it.

Say to yourself silently: "I am the Divine in human expression. My Divine Self has created me to be filled with well-being, abundance, success, love, and joy. My life is a cocreation between the

Divine and me. I have divine authority to manifest the fulfillment of all my desires, and I use this power rightly and wisely."

Continue to feel the energetic connection between your human self and your divine source, and let yourself be filled with the precise quality of energy you have been asking for. Imagine a white light coming down through the top of your head, radiating into and opening your heart, and filling up your power center, located two to three inches above your navel.

Breathe in this potent creative energy, knowing that it is magnetic in nature and has the power to draw to you the precise people, events, and experiences that will support the manifestation of your desire. And when you are ready, slowly and gently open your eyes.

To receive the Desire Factor Activity Guide and the Guided Meditation of all the energy mastery exercises offered throughout this book, please visit www.thedesirefactor.com/action.

2

The Principle of Focus

*As humans you have your personal free will and choice about
everything. How you exercise this free will is in your focus.
You are the director of your life experience in all aspects
and capacities. When you focus, you are not only in the
asking mode, but you are also directing where the
energy flows and what it flows to.*

The Quantum Council

Once a new desire has been born within us, there are only two
fundamental attitudes we can take in relation to it. We can
direct our attention to its absence and therefore continue to hold it
apart from us, or we can ponder, imagine, and delight in its eventual becoming, drawing it closer. The Principle of Focus highlights
the critical choice we all make in relation to each of our desires. We
have the power to choose either a path of struggle and resistance or
a path of joyful allowance. In other words, we can choose to relate
to our desires either from the vantage point of the divine energy

that creates all things or through our human eyes. These two primary perspectives are available to us in each situation, relationship, project, and condition we encounter. And which perspective we choose will determine how much ease or difficulty we experience in the realization of that desire.

The perspective of the energy stream that creates and sustains all things is always forward looking, possibility based, and solution oriented. It sees whatever situation that's before us as being rich with opportunities and resources that can be molded in each new moment in order to deliver us the precise experiences we've asked for. This part of us is always eager for what's next, and as a result, it naturally and easily attracts all cooperative energies, ideas, and resources to support our greatest joy. This is the part of us that knows that every person and every situation is a blank canvas, and that every color and texture under the rainbow is available for us to paint it in and to create our life experiences as we desire them to be.

In contrast to the divine perspective, there is also the human part of us that has been trained for most of our lives to scan for problems, to watch out for competition, to anticipate threats, and to view other people and life in general as a scarce and scary place. This is the part of us that focuses on limitations, dwells on past failures, and views other people as the reason we're being held back. It's the voice that often pipes up reflexively the moment we acknowledge something we desire and instantly shuts us down: *You'll never pull that off. What will people think? Who are you to want this anyway?* When a fresh new desire falls upon this path of doubt and resistance, the pure energy contained within it gets crushed across the rocks of our belief in our own limitations, and we do not receive the joy, expansion, or satisfaction that the desire has the potential to bring us. Instead, we struggle with our desires; we grow frustrated, resentful, and resigned when they do not manifest, and we blame the very situations and people whom we gave our creative power over to in the first place for the less-than-extraordinary lives we are living.

In every moment, and in relationship to every desire you hold, you must make a choice between these two radically different perspectives. The human perspective will likely come fairly easily because, after all, you're surrounded by other humans—most of whom don't know what you know about how the universe works. They still believe that mental and physical effort is what gets things done, so they work hard to accomplish the things they desire. They believe that in order to be wealthy, they have to manipulate someone else out of what they have already created. They see the resources of the world not as unlimited and continually replenished, but as one finite pie, in which everyone must fight to get their piece.

We are all born with free will, which means that at every moment we have the power to choose where and how to apply our most precious resource: the power of our focus. When we are determined to focus on the presence of our desire rather than its absence—when we are steadfast, resolved, and in harmony with the outcome we want—powerful forces come to our aid, and the energy that creates worlds flows in the direction of our choosing.

Being born with free will means, simply, that the divine energy of your desire can't impose itself on you because you have within you the power to allow it or to deny it. What does this mean in everyday terms? It means that if you're going to benefit from the divine perspective that knows that everything is energy and all things are possible, right now, then you're going to have to learn to focus on purpose.

Taking the Road Less Traveled

To apply the full power of your focus means that you're going to have to rise above the victim consciousness that most people are living inside of. You're going to have to spend less time *doing* and more time *imagining and feeling* your desired results into being. And I hate to break it to you, but you're probably going to have to give up, once and for all, your need to have others understand or agree with you. Chances are, most everyone you know is still going about life the hard way, and the more you try to convince them that there's an easier path, the more you'll deviate from your own center of power. You're only in charge of one trajectory, and it's the trajectory of your own desires. So I recommend you do yourself and others a big favor and apply your mental and emotional energy where it really counts.

In choosing the divine perspective, you're acknowledging that the energy you bring to any situation is what determines what that situation yields to you. You're reclaiming your power of influence by taking charge of your own vibrational offering. You're traveling a new path to the fulfillment of your desires, and this often means taking the road less traveled.

Think of it this way: The perspectives, beliefs, and chronic moods that you hold in relation to all things in your life are what make up your expectations. And your expectations are like well-traveled thought pathways within your consciousness, like deep grooves in a well-traveled road. If you travel that way often enough, you can get so habituated to that one path that you completely miss all the alternate roads you could take. And so, you keep on trucking down the same track, perhaps wondering why you keep getting the same results. The coworker who is "always" dismissive continues to show up that way for you—not because this is the only aspect of her personality that exists, but because this is just the vibe the two of you have going. We get what we expect, then use what turns up in our experience to validate our expectations.

There are two powerful categories in which each of us can make choices about how we direct the power of our focus in order to manifest our desires. I'll list these out for you here, and then we'll explore each one in depth.

- *You can choose to focus* . . . either on the abundant nature of the universe or on the evidence of lack you see in front of you.

- *You can choose to focus* . . . either ahead of time on what you want or after the fact on what happened.

Focusing on Abundance vs. Lack

When we focus from the perspective of lack, we are primarily aware that what we desire is missing, or is misbehaving, or is manifesting in a way that is more than, less than, or different than we'd like it to be. I call this a lack perspective because from this vantage point, we relate to our desire as something we need or want, because we don't yet have it. Another way of saying this is that we're coming from need and insufficiency, not from the expansive energy of pure desire.

Look, I get it. Wanting something from the perspective of not yet having it seems like a justified point of view, right? Because if you already had it—whatever it is—then you'd no longer want it. Although this is the relationship that most of the world has with their desires, I want you to understand that it's absolutely counterproductive to actually fulfilling yours. The act of wanting simply accentuates and produces more wanting. Noticing the absence of something only makes you more keenly aware of what's lacking. A far more powerful and productive way to relate to your desires is by focusing from the perspective of already having that which you want. You can get there by asking yourself a couple of simple questions:

- What do I believe the fulfillment of this desire will allow me to *have*?

- Who do I believe the fulfillment of this desire will allow me to *be*?

- How will the fulfillment of this desire cause me to *feel*?

By looking beyond *what* we want to the deeper desire of *why* we want it, we reconnect with the bottom-line feeling that we're really searching for—and what we discover is that this feeling is available to us right now. We don't need to postpone it until we arrive at some future destination. Let me give you a quick example.

I happen to love visiting model homes. I'm a huge fan of all things well-appointed and beautiful, and nothing fills my senses like seeing the work of a brilliant designer applying her creativity to something as essential as a living space. When I enter one of these homes, I drink in every detail. The high ceilings, the intentional use of color and texture, the crown moldings, the elegance of the faucets . . . I take it all in. For me, this experience is no different than being in a lush natural setting where my body is relaxed and my senses replenished by the beautiful sights and sounds. I have learned how to view designer homes through the focused lens of appreciation and abundance. I allow myself to be awed by the experience; I make mental notes of every design feature I love, and I leave each home feeling expanded, enlivened, and fulfilled.

But for someone unwittingly focused on lack, exploring model homes would evoke an entirely different reaction. The house tour would likely not be a foray into infinite possibilities but an excruciating incitement of unrealized potential. The opulence of the environment would only aggravate the experience of deprivation, eliciting feelings that range from yearning to downright despair.

Viewing life from the lens of lack and insufficiency is torturous. Not only do we deprive ourselves of the incredible benefit of aligning our energies with our desire, but we also deprive ourselves of the joy of the present moment. And the moment we make the choice to redirect our attention from what's missing externally to feeling the presence of abundance and appreciation within us, we shift our feeling state from wanting to *having*, from becoming to *being*, and from striving to *allowing* . . . and we change our point of attraction.

Our point of attraction—the degree to which our thoughts, beliefs, and emotions are in or out of alignment with our core desires—is the most powerful resource we have in every moment of our lives. It's like a lighthouse shining a signal that brings home every desire floating out there in the sea of pure potentiality—or prevents it from ever reaching the shore. Our point of attraction determines whether we generate upward momentum or downward spirals, whether we are met with open doors and green lights or detours and dead ends. When what we're attracting into our lives is not a reflection of what we really want, we alone have the power to change it, because we alone have the ability to change the direction of our focus.

Remember that the Law of Attraction is the manager of all the energy that flows into your experience. And that at their essence, everything and everyone that flows into your experience is made up of energy. There is an energetic tone to every relationship you're engaged in. The way your body looks, feels, and moves communicates a very unique energetic signature. There is an energetic frequency about the car you drive and within every material possession you own. The Law of Attraction does not mediate this flow of life energy based on what you say you want. It flows energy in response to how you *feel*. And there is a huge difference, vibrationally speaking, between the feeling of having and the feeling of yearning.

By focusing on the presence of all the ways you believe the manifestation of your desire will enhance your experience, you shift your perspective from wanting to having, from lack to abundance—and in so doing, you instantly turbocharge your power as a deliberate creator.

Focusing Ahead of Time vs. Reacting to the Past

In my book *Quantum Success: 7 Essential Laws for a Thriving, Joyful, and Prosperous Relationship with Work and Money*, I introduce the concept of creating an atmosphere within ourselves that is conducive to whatever result we desire to create. In other words, we decide who we want to be and how we want to feel before we ever walk into each new environment—and this practice really comes down to the power of our focus.

You don't need to wait until you're already in the middle of a particular interaction or situation and then simply react to the environment that's around you. Reacting to what's already happening diminishes so much of your creative power, it's like trying to lead from behind. Instead, you can decide in *advance* how you want to show up and how you want to feel, and then set yourself up to experience that in every way you can think of. You can be your own self-advocate, in the same way you would advocate for anyone you love.

For those of you who have kids, think back to their first day of preschool or kindergarten or summer camp. You didn't just roll up and drop them at the curb, did you? No. I'm guessing you put a lot of thought and intention into making sure that first-day experience would be a good one for them. In the weeks leading up to the event, you probably talked a lot about it and went out of your way to point out positive aspects of the experience that your child could look for and concentrate on. You may have used a countdown calendar or some other marker to help them get a feel for and become comfortable with the timeline. You may have even taken them shopping for some special trinket or toy, like a superhero lunchbox, that would be used only for that occasion in order to stoke their feelings of excitement. In other words, you helped them to focus positively toward the future event rather than just rolling into the experience without having done any of this important mental or emotional preparation.

Now, I know not everyone reading this book has or even desires children, so let's break down the art and practice of focusing ahead of time into a real-life situation that I know you'll be able to relate to.

Think about someone who you've had a difficult or contentious relationship with in the past. It could be a family member like a parent or an in-law, or even a neighbor. Let yourself dwell for one quick, hot minute on what you most don't like about your interactions with this person. And as you do, notice the momentum of those past experiences. Notice the emotions that are conjured within you just thinking about them. You may think you're just thinking about the past, but in fact, you are using the energy of the past to negatively create your present—and your future. Yikes! And to reverse this trend, you'll have to put as much mental and emotional energy into creating a more fulfilling experience.

I guided my friend Brenda through this process recently, and she chose to apply it in relation to her dad, whom she was about to spend a long weekend with. I asked her to briefly recall some past unpleasant encounters with her dad and to describe the emotional tone of them. Brenda's experience of her dad was that he is critical and stingy; that he talks only of himself and really does not have any interest in her or her two children. The more Brenda thought about her past experiences with her dad, the more animated she became—and the worse she felt. And, because she was only a couple of weeks away from seeing him for an extended period of time, she also began to conjure negative scenarios of how their time together might go down.

I asked Brenda to shake off those feelings, reminding her that she was the one generating them through the power of her focus and that she could just as easily choose to focus on something that made her feel better. I reminded her that her dad is a multifaceted human being capable of expressing the full range of human emotions, from stinginess to generosity; from selfish disinterest to total, interested engagement. And I told her that through the power of her focus, she could conjure a different experience of him that was far more in alignment with what she truly desires. After she was breathing a little easier, we continued.

I then asked Brenda to do her best to leave her past experiences of her dad out of her current point of focus and to answer this

question: If the upcoming weekend with your dad were to go exactly the way you desire it to, how would you feel? With this question, we shifted her focus from critically remembering all the things she didn't like about their past interactions to softly thinking about what she'd like to experience in the future.

Words like *lighthearted* and *fun* came to Brenda's mind. She envisioned her upcoming visit with her dad to be free-flowing and comfortable. She imagined them taking walks, looking through pictures, laughing a lot, and enjoying the simple process of cooking Thanksgiving dinner together. I asked her to share some of her dad's most positive aspects that might easily lend to them enjoying one another's company, and she was able to easily name quite a few.

She told me her dad is funny and creative and that he must care deeply about her and her children because he went to great lengths to make sure all of his affairs are in order so as not to leave any type of burden for her. She remembered back to her childhood and all the efforts her dad had made to remain a part of her life despite being estranged from her mother. In a matter of just a few short minutes, Brenda's feelings about her father had softened and she was genuinely looking forward to their time together. By opening up a space within her for a new experience to take root, she took a very important first step toward creating what she desired instead of re-creating what she didn't want.

Beyond this initial conversation with me, Brenda made some further preparations of her own energy field in advance of her trip. She didn't just show up at her dad's door hauling her same old worn-out set of beliefs and expectations. Instead, she practiced the feelings that she wanted to experience well ahead of time, and on the day she began her trip, she made sure she gave herself the necessary time and space to get herself mentally, emotionally, and energetically receptive to this experience.

But the most important tool that Brenda brought to the table was that of accountability. She gave up all the justifications and excuses she'd been using for years to explain the unsatisfying relationship she had with her dad. She gave up the perception that her dad was "just that way," and took 100 percent responsibility for creating the type of experience with him that she wanted. She consciously saw her dad as a cooperative participant in this experience, reminding herself that he, too, wanted to have a good relationship with her.

Then, on the day she arrived, relaxed and energized, she used the power of her focus to imagine and look forward to how the next few days of their time together would unfold. In other words, she set herself up to win before she ever set foot in her dad's house. As a direct result of Brenda's sharpened focus and clear intentions, she and her dad enjoyed more laughs and moments of lightness than they had in many years.

Feeling Forward

When you lovingly give your energy and positive attention to something in the process of becoming—in the same way a farmer tends his freshly planted crop or a pregnant woman joyfully anticipates the baby she will one day hold in her arms—you are actually training your mind to reach beyond the circumstances you are currently living in to generate the feeling state of the essence of your desire. And on the other hand, if at any time you tunnel your focus to include only the reality that has already assembled around you—the exact number of dollars in your bank account, for example, or the number of clients you've served to date—you are limiting the astounding creative power of your thoughts and emotions. To unleash your full creative potential, you need to focus forward, beyond what currently is, and toward the reality that is in the process of coming into being.

This may sound esoteric, but really, it's no different than throwing a successful dinner party! Think about it: As the host or hostess, you decide who you want to assemble based on the chemistry, interests, and potential synergy of each person within the group. You take charge of the type of meal you're going to make. You gather the necessary ingredients and give yourself plenty of time to enjoy preparing them. On the day of the event, you do things that put you in a good mood, and you may even enhance the beauty of your home with candles or fresh flowers. And, if you're already a skilled, deliberate creator, you begin thinking thoughts of appreciation about everyone who will join you that evening and making a mental list of their points of harmony and positive aspects. In other words, if you were hosting a dinner party, you'd take 100 percent accountability for creating the environment you want your guests to walk into ahead of time. Perfectly logical, right?

And yet, how many times do we forego this important preparation in order to check one more thing off the to-do list? How often do we rush out the door to pick up the kids—and then get angry when they reflect back to us our internal state of frenzy or crankiness? How many times do we drag ourselves into the car for the holiday work party with a *let's get this over with* mentality? And how many times does the result harmonize perfectly with the negative expectations we hold? This is mis-creating, folks. And there's just no way to sugarcoat it.

It's easy to think thoughts like, *Oh, he's just a negative person* or *This doctor always runs late.* Or *I have a slow metabolism* or *The spark has gone out of my marriage.* But remember that nothing in life is simply "the way it is." Every molecule that is called into being is activated by the attention of the observer. If you change your expectation, you'll change your experience.

The question here is not whether you're justified in holding negative expectations about what's about to unfold. I'm sure there are plenty of areas of your life where you'd be justified in expecting a negative outcome—in the same way Brenda's past experiences provided plenty of excuses to continue to focus negatively about her dad. The only relevant question is, Do you like the results your expectation is yielding to you? And if you don't, know that you can do something about it. Not by lamenting the past, but by focusing forward.

This river of life-giving creative energy that sources all things flows only in one direction, and that direction is forward. To keep up with it and work in partnership with it, you also have to be forward looking and feeling. So never mind beating up on yourself over the ten pounds you've gained or the credit card debt you racked up over the holidays. Never mind rehashing the fight you had with your spouse—unless you're keen to create another one! There is no value whatsoever in looking back.

When to Focus Generally, and When to Be Specific

So what's the most productive thing to do when you realize you've been mis-creating? What if you haven't been forward looking or focusing on solutions but have been dwelling on problems instead? What if you've been focusing on lack rather than abundance? What if you look around some particular area of your life and notice that most of it is not how you'd like it to be? This is where the practice of focusing on your desire in general terms comes in.

There is a big misconception out there that deliberate creating means having to visualize in very specific terms exactly what we want to create. We make vision boards made of images of ourselves in size 4 bathing suits, tanning on the beaches of Tahiti, or holding hands with the man or woman of our dreams. And all of this is well and good, *if*—and there's a really big *if* here—*if* visualizing, fantasizing, or using affirmations feels good to you when you do it. If it's delicious to envision your desire in all its three-dimensional detail, or if trotting out to the Jaguar dealership to smell the leather of your dream car gets your juices flowing, then by all means do those things and do them often!

But if those things don't feel good to you, if doing them conjures thoughts like *Who am I kidding?* or *How will I possibly accomplish this?*, if these practices lead you down the dead-end road of thinking about failed relationships or unmet goals gone by, then you need to take this as a giant red light to stop. Because in this case, getting specific is working against you.

Anytime you are focused on something and it does not feel good to you, it means only one thing. In that particular moment, and in relation to that particular desire, you are focused more upon lack than you are on abundance. You're more aware of its absence than you are of its becoming, or you're focused upon the situation as it is and not on how you'd prefer it to be. In this instance, you are using the powerful lens of your attention to resist the very outcome you desire, and in so doing, you are working against yourself.

The whole point of this chapter is to help you see that your mind is a focusing mechanism. Through the power of your focus, you send out a signal that the entire universe is responding to. And you can tell by the way you feel whether your focus is bringing you closer to what you desire or taking you farther away from it. The skill of knowing when to focus in on something specifically and when to back off and become more general is one that can be honed only by paying really close attention to how you feel—by caring about how you feel above all things, in fact. And when you find that your specific focus is making you feel worse instead of better, back away from the ledge!

So if thinking about winning the lottery lights you up and makes your imagination run wild, then by all means, think about it. But the moment your thoughts tip in the direction of calculating the odds or remembering all the times you felt disappointed to have missed the winning number, it's time to jump that train and sit beside the track for a moment until the momentum of it passes you by. Or better yet, allow your mind to wander off the subject altogether.

Focusing the mind generally has many advantages. When you think in general terms, you are less likely to introduce resistance. Your mind is less likely to become attached to any particular avenue through which you believe whatever you desire will flow, and is better able to remain open to the fact that there are multiple channels through which it can flow, most of which we can't even imagine from our vantage point in any given moment.

But focusing specifically also has its advantages. The more specific our focus, the more energy we summon toward our desire. When our specific focus is unobstructed by the resistance of doubt or fear, focusing on something we want and filling in all the details is fun and life-giving and exciting. Let me give you an example.

Overall, my husband, Frederic, is much more general and laid-back in his focus than I am. When each New Year approaches and I ask him things like "What do you want to experience in the coming year?" inevitably his answers are very general in nature. He'll say things like "I want to keep experiencing joy with you and the boys" or "I want to continue feeling happy and vital and alive." But that same question, directed to me, always yields much more specific answers. When I look forward toward each New Year, or even toward a new segment of my day, my mind instantly and easily shows me detailed pictures of what I want to create. In fact, the question "What do you want?" in and of itself is one of the fastest ways to get my creative juices flowing.

When I focus this question in the area of my business, new programs unfold in my mind and books practically write themselves in my head. If I focus that question toward my family and children, I'm flooded with images and ideas for how to expand the happiness in our already happy family. When I think about what I want in terms of my own self-expression and joy, I also get in touch with very specific desires—and of course, those desires are consistent with who I am, the life that I've lived, and the things that I uniquely enjoy. Purses and heels and spa days, oh my!

One of the things I love to do is watch dance shows, because dancing is like art to me. It's amazing to see people so talented move their bodies to the music, and because I used to be a dancer, I can appreciate the level of athleticism that it takes to do what they do. And I'm a particularly huge fan of the TV show *Dancing with the Stars*. Frederic and I often watch the show together, both because he appreciates seeing new dance moves and also because he loves watching any type of expression of joy.

So a couple of years ago, Frederic gave me tickets to see the *Dancing with the Stars* tour as a Christmas gift, which included a VIP meet-and-greet event with the dancers before the show. As we were driving to the event, I was looking at the flyer that featured pictures of all twelve of the dancers (six women and six men) and I asked him, "Out of all twelve of these dancers, who do you most want to meet?" Frederic thought about it for a moment, then responded, "I want to meet all of them."

"No, I mean who do you *really* want to see?" I clarified, naturally wanting to get more specific because I knew it would enhance my excitement. "Out of all of them, who is your top person?" Again, he answered, "I don't have one. I would be happy seeing any of them." Now, understanding the differences between how Frederic and I approach the art of manifestation, and knowing that he creates amazing results by being general while I enjoy creating more specifically, I accepted his general answers, but in response I told him that my desire was to meet two of my favorite dancers. For those of you familiar with the show, their names are Gleb and Keo. We left it at that—Frederic with his general desire to enjoy the experience in whatever way it would unfold and me with my specific desire to see my very favorite dancers—and continued driving to the show.

We walked through the VIP meet-and-greet, where we did get to meet two of the dancers and spent about a minute with each of them. After that experience was over, realizing we still had about an hour and a half before the show started, we decided to take a walk to get something to eat. As we left the venue and walked outside, we were greeted by one of the most spectacular sunsets ever to light up the Phoenix sky. I took out my cell phone and turned away from Frederic momentarily to snap some pics. And as I was looking at the photos, I heard my husband from behind me, almost yelling, say, "There is no way we are *not* going to take a picture with you!"

I looked up and there were . . . Gleb and Keo!

In the work I do, I meet a lot of celebrities. As a matter of fact, I coach a lot of celebrities. But in the moment of meeting those two, in such a completely spontaneous way, I felt like a starstruck schoolgirl. The combination of Frederic's general focus and my very specific desire was the perfect blend for manifestation. I would suggest that this combination, when used intentionally, is always a winning formula.

Learning to consciously direct the power of your focus is a skill that has to be developed and requires continued practice because it flies in the face of how most of us were taught to relate to the world. But this is the only way we can refine our awareness as to when something feels good and choose to move forward in that direction, and similarly to know when something feels bad and make the powerful choice to abandon ship.

Remember that once a new desire has been born within you, there are only two basic positions you can take in relation to it. You can focus on either its lack or its abundance. You can make either the absence or the presence of what you desire foremost in your mind. You can focus on the feeling of wanting it, missing it, or worrying about it, or on the sensation of already having and appreciating it. With the power of your focus, you can zoom in to any experience of reality you desire. You can include every detail, or you can completely blur the lines. You can use your powerful mind to find fault or to look for things to praise. You can observe what's missing, or you can appreciate all that you already have. And whatever reality you direct your focus toward, just know that that reality will expand.

To begin applying the Principle of Focus, the only guide you need to consult is the way you feel. Different types of focus will serve you at different times and in relation to different desires. Allow your emotions to be your guide, and let your mind be the servant to that master. What you are going for is to once again reconnect with that feeling of unrestricted, unobstructed desire that you probably experienced as a child. Your goal is to be at peace with where you are and to be in a state of joyful expectancy about all that's to come.

Chapter 2: The Principle of Focus—
Applying It Step by Step

1   As you call to mind your current Desire Factor, notice to what extent your daily thoughts and choices oppose your wanting and therefore set you upon a path of greater resistance. In what ways are you pulling in opposition to what you want? Where and how are you applying too much effort in an attempt to overcome resistance?

2   And now, in relation to this same Desire Factor, notice and acknowledge where, how, and in what ways you are excellent at receiving and allowing. What enhances your sense of faith and supports you in being more allowing? In this area of your life, what makes you happy? What are you supremely thankful for? What future images do you contemplate about this desire that give you genuine present-moment pleasure when you contemplate them? Take a few moments to play and replay through your mind all the ways in which you are allowing of and in alignment with your Desire Factor, acknowledging that what you focus on expands and becomes more in your experience.

3 Acknowledge that in every moment, there are an infinite number of things and experiences that you can choose to give your attention to. The universe is your own personal treasure chest, stocked by the divine storehouse within you, and through the power of your focus, you can expand your consciousness to accept all the good that is available and waiting for you.

4 Choose today to focus the power of your attention on the things, circumstances, situations, and experiences that you deeply desire, knowing that what you focus on expands and becomes more. Focus always on the presence of what you want, and withdraw your attention from the unwanted. The following exercise will help you do that.

Energy Mastery Exercise

Feeling Forward in the Direction of Your Desire

Begin by closing your eyes and allowing your body to find a position of comfort and ease. Breathe deeply, feeling your breath traveling throughout your physical body. Follow the rhythm of it as it moves easily in and out. And notice that your breath is actually a vehicle that connects your physical body with your energy body or aura, and by placing your gentle awareness on your breath, you naturally begin to raise your consciousness to the more subtle dimensions of your being . . . to the source or wellspring of all physical manifestations.

As you continue giving yourself the gift of your undivided attention, feel yourself letting go, surrendering any stress from your day, and bringing the full presence of yourself into this moment. Your thoughts are becoming clearer, quieter, and subtler. Your emotions are calm and serene.

And now begin to gently bring to mind something you want to manifest. Take a moment to consider this, because the process we are about to do will magnetize it to you. It might be something tangible, like a relationship or a new car. It could be an accomplishment, such as writing a book or completing a project. Or it could be something subtle and less tangible, such as feeling happier or more inspired for no logical reason. Identify this desire in terms as specific or as general as feels right for you. Breathe into this outcome that you desire, allowing the image, the experience, and the feeling of it to become clearer.

Remind yourself that you are the director of your life experience in all aspects and capacities, and that your focus is the means for exercising this incredible power. When you focus, you direct the energy that creates worlds toward whatever reality you wish to create. Just breathe that in. You are *that* powerful.

As you continue to contemplate this object or experience that you desire, notice any ways in which your thoughts or feelings about it are convoluted or conflicted. Do your best not to judge this, for it is neither permanent nor necessary. Negative thoughts, beliefs, or feelings simply mean that you have split energy toward your desire. A part of you wants it, and another part of you doubts your ability to create it. The key to bridging this gap lies in your determination to deliberately direct your focus in ways that bring you a feeling of relief, of acceptance, of relaxation.

With another deep breath, ask yourself, How does the infinite, divine, all-powerful part of me think and feel about the object of my desire? Notice that the larger part of you feels no doubt, no frustration, no negativity. Only enthusiasm and passion about your desire. Use your breath to experience these feelings fully. Allow the divine perspective to penetrate your mind, your perceptions, your expectations.

Take a moment to acknowledge to yourself that focusing on a perception of lack always feels bad, and focusing on the presence of abundance always feels good. And you always have the choice—thanks to the power of your own free will—on where to focus your attention. Give yourself permission to bring the vibration of your thoughts, feelings, expectations, and beliefs in line with and up to speed with the vibration of your desire.

Remember that the river of life-giving creative energy that sources all things flows only in one direction, and that direction is forward. Make a commitment to yourself now to flow your personal energy in the direction that the larger stream is flowing and to direct your all-powerful focus toward your desire, which is even now in the process of becoming.

Take another few moments in silence to enjoy the benefits of deliberately applying the Principle of Focus. Allow the cascade of good-feeling emotions to continue washing over you, refreshing you and recalibrating your point of attraction. And when you are ready, slowly begin to stretch, to wiggle your fingers and toes, and to become aware of the room you are in. And when you are ready, gently open your eyes, bringing this new, more refined perspective into the next beautiful segment of your day.

3

The Principle of Joyful Expectancy

*Because you create from your own personal awareness and
knowledge of what is possible and probable, when you decide
what you desire and allow the flow of pure positive energy to
move through you toward that desire, that will then become your
experience in the physical. Forms are always created by the
energy first, and your expectations and beliefs are the shaping
of that energy into form. What you expect . . . you get.*

The Quantum Council

*Y*ou now understand that energy is the "stuff" that everything
"in the universe"—including you, me, plants, animals, and
even inanimate objects that we interact with in our daily lives—
is made of. And you understand that the universal energy that
creates and sustains all things responds, in precise measure, to the
energy you offer through the power of your focus. Where your
attention goes, energy flows, and energy is the foundation of

everything—whether material or immaterial—that you could possibly desire.

Up to this point, however, our exploration about how manifestations take place has been a little theoretical. You might accept that your attention to things, both wanted and unwanted, attracts more of those things into your experience, and yet, how exactly can you know what you're in the process of attracting? You know that your thoughts generate vibrations, and those vibrations gather other resonant vibrations, but you probably aren't aware of the vibrational nature of your most dominant or habitual thoughts. In actuality, there's really no possible way you can sort out every thought—especially given that scientists have now estimated that the average person thinks about sixty thousand thoughts every single day. Likewise, I'm sure you're conscious of the wide range of feelings you experience in any given day, but how do those feelings contribute to what does or doesn't manifest in your life?

At this point I hope that you're starting to get a sense of the incredibly powerful vibrational being that you are. Each of us is like this highly sophisticated, high-powered machine, and in every waking moment we are broadcasting a frequency that the Law of Attraction is responding to. But where exactly is the owner's manual for this amazing machine, and how can you become more sensitive to, and masterful about, the vibrations you are offering? The answer to these all-important questions is this: Each of us was born with a highly accurate, extremely sensitive gauge that lets us know moment by moment what we are emanating vibrationally. That gauge is our emotions. And where we stand—emotionally and vibrationally—in relation to our desires has everything to do with how quickly they manifest in our experience.

In this chapter, we'll look at the vital role that your emotions play in helping you to distinguish where you are in relation to your Desire Factor, how to interpret the messages your emotions are sending you, and—ultimately—how to generate positive, receptive, creative feeling states on purpose. So let's dive deep into the world of your emotions, because mastering this realm provides the fastest path to mastering deliberate manifestation.

The Vibrational Range of Emotions

As a conscious human being who's had twenty, forty, or sixty or more years' experience of circling the sun, you innately understand that you are capable of feeling a huge spectrum of emotions. And you also know that your emotions can sometimes swing very suddenly, even without much obvious provocation. The emotional realm of life may seem random or chaotic, but I assure you it is neither of those things. Like everything else in the universe, your emotions can be understood in terms of their vibrational nature.

Learning to correlate each emotion you experience with its unique vibrational frequency gives you far more than just an understanding of the feeling state you're experiencing on any given day. It gives you a moment-by-moment window into how in sync you are with the energy that creates worlds (the Principle of Alignment), where and how you are directing your attention (the Principle of Focus), and what you are right now—by virtue of your focus—in the process of creating (the Principle of Joyful Expectancy). Emotional extremes such as fear or eagerness, tension or relief, confusion or clarity are neither good nor bad; they are simply messengers that bring us valuable insight regarding where we stand in relation to whatever it is we want to create. Our emotional reactions—both positive and negative—provide moment-by-moment information about whether we are energetically aligned with, or in opposition to, the outcomes we desire.

Anytime we have a desire that is associated with even the slightest bit of angst—if we want something but doubt in our ability to get it, if we have something and are in fear of losing it, if we've attracted something but won't allow it to continue to evolve—our experience is one of dissatisfaction. Life is designed to keep expanding, and to live a fulfilling life, we simply have to become active participants in our own expansion. And this means we have to keep bringing our vibration into harmony with our ever-expanding desires.

To find out whether the vibration you are sending out is attracting or repelling the outcomes that you desire, you need only to pay attention to the way you feel. Your emotions are like guideposts that tell you whether the vibration you are emitting in each changing moment is in alignment with the expanded or the contracted version of yourself. Generally speaking, when we feel good, we are in an energy field of abundance. When we feel bad, we are in an energy field of lack. The better we feel, the more allowing, receptive, and expectant we are of our desires unfolding naturally; the worse we feel, the more resistance we're offering and the harder those desires will be to attain. Emotions are simply energy in motion, and like the keys on a piano, each one vibrates at a particular frequency.

Over the years, there have been many teachers, scientists, psychologists, and researchers who have attempted to classify or quantify emotions in terms of their vibrational frequency. Scientology's L. Ron Hubbard introduced the idea in 1951, when he created an emotional tone scale intended to assess how "alive" or "dead" someone is in a spiritual or vibrational sense. Fifty years later, psychiatrist David R. Hawkins's book *Power vs. Force* published the results of thousands of studies conducted using kinesiology, which classified the range of human emotions on a frequency scale from one to one thousand. More recently, Law of Attraction teachers Esther and Jerry Hicks developed what they call an Emotional Guidance Scale, published in their 2004 book, *Ask and It Is Given*. Other researchers, like the folks at HeartMath, have correlated the vibrational frequency of certain emotions with particular hertz frequency rates.

These are all great resources, and I highly encourage you to check them out if you're so inspired. But after twenty years of studying, practicing, and teaching the art and science of energy mastery, I've come up with a way of understanding the frequency of emotions that I believe simplifies it all.

Your Emotional Continuum

As we've already discussed, your emotions run along a spectrum of frequency, and—like the spectrum of light frequencies in a rainbow—they move along a continuum from denser, more resistant energies to those that are progressively more subtle and free-flowing. At the high end of your emotional spectrum are good-feeling emotions like joy, appreciation, empowerment, freedom, and love. And at the opposite end of the continuum, we dip into the range of horrible-feeling emotions like shame, despair, grief, depression, and hopelessness. In fact, these vibrations are so slow-moving in terms of their energetic frequency that we actually feel paralyzed when we experience them.

When we're vibrating on the good-feeling end of this emotional spectrum, our perspective related to all things is one of abundance, elation, appreciation, and—yes—joyful expectancy. We are perfectly in tune with the source energy that creates and sustains all things, and feeling fabulous is a natural byproduct of this internal state of alignment. We know ourselves to be infinite, energetic beings who are in constant contact with the energy that creates worlds, and as such, we're naturally receptive to ideas, solutions, inspirations, and beneficial courses of action.

When we're attuned to the high-flying end of the emotional scale, we are resilient and clear minded, and our immunity to criticism, confusion, and self-doubt is extremely high. Good luck seems to follow us wherever we go, resources reveal themselves around every corner, and obstacles either rarely arise or are easily overcome. We're in the right place at the right time, and we move through the world in a state of ease and flow, or what some call grace. Because we're in an internal state of alignment with our broader selves, we feel more beautiful and fluid in our bodies than usual. We feel invincible, and we joyfully anticipate positive outcomes and pleasurable experiences wherever we go. And the universe—our devoted, receptive, cocreative energy partner—yields those experiences to us in easy and seemingly magical ways.

And when on the other hand, our emotions are vibrating in the lower, slower, denser frequencies along this emotional spectrum, it is because we are focusing on lack, dwelling on problems, and zooming in on current circumstances that do not please us. And this focus both brings to light and accentuates all the internal and external resistance that is opposing our desires. We see other people or outside circumstances as obstacles to our happiness, and in so doing, we deprive ourselves of our inherent power to improve our mood and alter the conditions of our lives. We're quick to feel anger and frustration, and—in our extreme dissatisfaction—we seek to assign blame either on another or on ourselves for how badly we're feeling.

When we're focused on lack, we easily spiral into black-and-white thinking, and even aspects of our lives that we're generally happy with suddenly appear hopeless or insufficient. And even though we're in a state of heightened discomfort, we cannot seem to find the motivation to pull ourselves out of it. We resist going for that walk, taking a few deep breaths, or stepping away from the situation completely. Nope. In those moments, falling into self-destructive habits and tendencies seems like a much better idea. We give in to the temptation to gossip, complain, and criticize. We head out to the mall to buy one more thing we really don't need. We reach for food to comfort us even though we're not hungry or a stiff drink to "take the edge off," even though it's only four in the afternoon.

The vibrational frequency of lack is at the root of all vices. We know at the deepest level of our beings that we are supposed to feel good, but when we're feeling these lower vibrations, we're temporarily cut off from all the benevolence of the universe. All the energy that creates worlds is still flowing to us and through us, available to support us in the fulfillment of all our desires, but our lack-filled thinking has us standing behind our own self-constructed walls. And so even though these resources are being showered upon us, we are in no state to receive them.

At the very center of these two vibrational extremes is an emotional state of being that can be described as neutrality, as acceptance, willingness, contentment, or—as I will refer to it throughout this book—a state of sufficiency. This is the midline, the fulcrum, the tipping point between the lower realms where we can only create experiences of lack, insufficiency, and greater suffering and the higher realms where we are open to receiving abundance and well-being in all its many forms. In later chapters, we'll talk in much greater detail about the importance of finding the vibration of sufficiency—and precisely how to go about doing it. For now, I just want you to get a visceral sense of how good-feeling emotions are what we experience when we are focused on the upper register of our emotional scale, and how bad-feeling emotions are what we experience when we allow ourselves to dwell in the vibration of lack.

So, as you can see, it's no fun whatsoever hanging out on the resistant end of the infinite vibrational energy stream—especially once you know that you could just as easily be having an experience of supreme ease and flow. It's a little like dog-paddling through thick, heavy mud when all the while you could be swimming in a clear, pristine, crystalline pool at the other end of the lake. But the good news is, once you know these two radically different experiences of life are available to you in every moment, you can begin navigating yourself deliberately in the direction of your Desire Factor. And your emotions—both good-feeling and bad-feeling—serve as your constant compass, letting you know whether you're on track toward manifesting everything you want or you're straying off course. Because however you are feeling right now about the object of your desire is setting the stage for the future experiences that will unfold between you and it.

If you're worrying, doubtful, or angry, you're actively planning for an unsatisfying future experience. If you're eager, appreciative, and joyful, you're using your creative power to plan, prepare, and ready yourself to receive a future that will delight you. As Albert Einstein so brilliantly said, "Imagination is everything. It is the preview of life's coming attractions." Remember that the Law of Attraction was never designed to bring you what you want. It is designed to bring you what you expect—in the form of people, circumstances, and experiences.

The Expectation Effect

The word *expect* comes from the Latin word *expectare*, which has two parts. Ex means "thoroughly," and *spectare* means "to look." So if we define the word literally, to expect something is to actively, thoroughly, and intently look for that which we already believe exists. Whatever we look for, we are likely to find. Why? Because in the very act of flowing energy toward that potential outcome, we are magnetically attracting it into our life. In his book, *Working with the Law*, originally published back in 1964, Dr. Raymond Holliwell writes, "Desire connects you with the thing desired and expectation draws it into your life."

When we expect a certain outcome to unfold, whether that outcome is something we desire or dread, our brains sort the trillions of pieces of data that are coming at us in every given moment and then filter into our perception only those that are in harmony or resonance with our expectations. This is Law of Attraction 101, and even though this exact phrase is somewhat new, scientists have been studying this phenomenon for decades.

In 1968, psychology professors Robert Rosenthal and Lenore Jacobson conducted an experiment, at the University of California, Riverside, to test the degree to which teachers' expectations of students had the power to impact those students' academic performance. In this experiment, elementary school teachers were told that a certain group of students in their classrooms had performed exceptionally well on a test that predicts academic "blooming" and, as a result, were expected to make significant academic gains in the coming year. And sure enough, within just a few short months, that group of students had indeed outperformed the other students.

In reality, there was no such test that predicted academic blooming. The children who had been presented to the teachers as gifted and on the precipice of blooming intellectually were selected randomly and had previously demonstrated a huge range in terms of academic aptitude. What produced the dramatic difference in these students' achievements, according to Professor Rosenthal, was "the mind-set and expectations of the teacher."

"Expectation becomes a self-fulfilling prophecy," Rosenthal went on to say. "When teachers have been led to expect better intellectual performance from their students, they tend to get it. When coaches are led to expect better athletic performance from their athletes, they tend to get it. When behavioral researchers are led to expect a certain response from their research subjects, they tend to get it."[*] In other words, positive expectations summon an energy field that makes the intended outcome that much easier to achieve.

Years later, Dr. Norman Vincent Peale—affectionately known as the Father of Positive Thinking—conducted his own annual experiment on the power of expectation. Each New Year's Eve, Dr. Peale would ask the members of his church to write down one expectation they held for themselves for the year ahead and to seal it in an envelope, which they would open the following New Year's Eve. When the group gathered one year later, the members were surprised to discover that their expectations, for the most part, had come true.

One man, a student of astrology, had recently read that the coming year would be a difficult time for Capricorns and that they could expect to lose their marriage partners, their jobs, or both. This prediction became the man's expectation, and one year later, his reality. He had lost both during the same year. Another member of the same group—who, interestingly enough, was also a Capricorn—had written down that she expected to receive a job promotion in the coming year. But unlike the first member's, her expectation was

---

[*] Quoted in Sharon Begley's article "Expectations May Alter Outcomes Far More Than We Realize," *The Wall Street Journal Online*, November 7, 2003.

not tainted by any cryptic astrological predictions, and she joyfully attracted a job promotion. Yet another member of the church group had passed away earlier in the year. When the group opened his envelope, his message read, "No member of my family has ever lived past sixty, so I expect to die next year." He did.

Holding an expectation that contradicts our desires is like trying to reach a mountain peak by traveling downhill. It just can't be done. We move in the direction we're facing, and that direction has everything to do with how much joy, abundance, and success we expect to come our way.

Expectation vs. Desire

Remember that we live in a world where energy, not matter, is the primary force behind all creation. Expectation generates a powerfully attractive energy, which—though invisible—is every bit as real as electricity. The expectations you hold in relation to each of your desires create an atmosphere, like a weather pattern or climate, which you carry with you everywhere you go. If you've ever known someone who seems to bring sunshine everywhere they go, or someone who always has a dark cloud of negativity over their head, then you innately have an understanding of the power of expectation. And the power of expectation can work to our advantage or to our detriment. I worked with a coaching client recently who created an unconscious expectation early in her life that continued to sabotage her success well into her adult years.

As a little girl, Lori was abused by her mom and never received the kind of love, attention, or approval that she desperately desired. Then, when Lori was four years old, she became very ill with pneumonia. Her mom, who was usually short-tempered, distracted, and neglectful, suddenly became loving and attentive, doting all over her daughter until she recovered from the illness. Lori made the connection from that very early age that in order to get the things she desired, she would have to get sick.

As a grown woman, Lori had a desire to quit her high-paying corporate job in order to invest in her own business, but she wasn't sure how to go about accomplishing that. Shortly thereafter, she was involved in a work-related car accident that awarded her plenty of money to begin her new venture but left her injured. Once again, she got what she wanted, but—consistent with that deep-seated expectation—it was at the expense of her health and well-being.

I share this story to illustrate the power of expectation. We get what we expect—whether it's wanted or unwanted, conscious or unconscious, by deliberate intent or by default. Expectation is a force—or maybe it's more accurate to describe it as a force field. When we offer an expectation, we draw to ourselves all people, situations, and experiences that match it while repelling those that don't. I really want you to get a visual of this.

Remember what we explored in the first chapter, that what we call "reality" is nothing more than formless particles that take shape in response to the energy we offer through our attention? Well, our chronic expectations carry a powerful energy that determines which particles do, and don't, make their way into our experience. If your desire is to call forth greater financial prosperity but your chronic expectation is that the economy is bad, or that no one with your level of education makes it big, or that your talents are underappreciated, those expectations form a kind of energetic wall that will block your prosperity from getting in. You just cannot complain about what currently is *and* be in a state of receptivity to what you'd prefer. If you feel disadvantaged, unimportant, or unwelcome, you are radiating a vibration that is interfering with your openness to the very situations you want to change.

Think for a moment about the energy of your heartfelt desire. What is the vibrational frequency of the beautiful, fit, flexible body you desire? What is the vibration of security, or of enjoying huge streams of lavish financial abundance? How does it feel to be engaged in intimate, connected, easy relationships with those you love? It's important to understand that every single time a desire for those things arises within you, you send out a powerful vibrational request that the universe hears, receives, and is responding to.

The question is, Is the energy of your expectations in vibrational proximity to the energy of those desires? If it is, those desires are manifesting easily into your life experience. If not, then they're taking more time, energy, and angst than is necessary for—or beneficial to—their unfolding. And the more life we live in the absence of what we really desire, the more solidified and justified our expectations become—which is a self-fulfilling prophecy that holds apart from us all that we're striving to manifest.

There is really only one way to bridge the gap between what you want and what you currently have, and I'm just going to give it to you straight. You must decide to lean in the direction of where you're going, not to dwell in where you've been. Choose to reside on the good-feeling end of the emotional scale, on the side of faith and assurance. Choose to believe that the best is yet to come. Choose to remind yourself every single day that you are the point of attraction to which the entire universe is responding and that you always, in each new moment, have the power to start fresh. Choose to see the best in others and in yourself. Choose to use the incredible power of your imagination to paint the picture of things turning out well and to use the incredible power of your emotions to deliberately conjure the corresponding joyful feeling state of having created all that you want. Optimism is like sunshine for the mind. It promotes life, beauty, and growth, and it draws to it more of the same. As Neville Goddard, the spiritual luminary and twentieth-century author, wrote in his 1961 book, *The Law and the Promise*, "If you long . . . to transform your present life into a dream of what might well be, you need but imagine that you are already what you want to be and to feel the way you would expect to feel under such circumstances." Great advice! Let's dive into how this might play out on a day-to-day basis.

The Art of Joyful Expectancy

Think about all the action-oriented preparations you typically make in the areas of your life in which you are really committed to bringing about a positive outcome. Think of all the things you do for your children, the acts of service you provide for your spouse, the things you organize or purchase for the sake of enhancing the beauty and functionality of your household. Consider the many hours you spend planning, shopping for, and dressing for just one special occasion, or the lengths you go to in order to make birthdays and holidays extra special for your loved ones.

This is not a theoretical exercise. I actually want you to consider the action hours that you invest in the aspects of your life where you're committed to having your desires fulfilled. If it's easier, you can think of this in terms of time spent on a weekly basis. Now, in relation to that number of hours, I want you to consider how much time, attention, and energy you spend investing in adjusting your expectations to match the outcome you're hoping to achieve.

You may spend four hours a week at the gym, but how much of that time are you actually joyfully expecting and feeling appreciation for the results you wish to achieve? You might spend six hours a week cooking, cleaning, or doing laundry, but consider for just a moment the expectations you're nourishing mentally and energetically while you're engaged in those tasks. Are you enlivening your appreciation for the fact that your children are growing more and more autonomous and responsible all the time? Are you loving your home and the fact that you are strong and flexible enough to clean it? Are you nourishing the expectation of you and your spouse falling deeper and deeper in love?

When you're buying new furniture, balancing your checkbook, or preparing paperwork for your accountant, what is your dominant expectation? Is it an expectation that resources are dwindling or that you will of course continue to ride bigger and bigger waves of abundance? Expectation matters, folks. It's not about the actions we take. It's about the energy we cultivate within us and then infuse into those actions. That's what moves worlds. For better or for worse, this universe responds to our energy, which means to summon its full creative power we have to be emotionally, energetically, vibrationally invested in the fulfillment of what we desire. We can't just phone this in!

There is tremendous, momentous power in expectation, and yet, we often don't regard it as such because it's subtle. It's invisible. But expectation is more powerful in terms of summoning and directing energy than any action we can take. When I was eight and a half months pregnant with my youngest son, Maxim, I went in for my weekly checkup with my doctor and learned that he was in a transverse position, meaning that his body was lying side to side in my womb rather than positioned headfirst in the birth canal. She explained that to deliver in this position would be very dangerous for me and for Maxim, and she told me that because my due date was just ten days away, I needed to schedule a procedure for the very next day when she would attempt to maneuver him manually into the proper position. She explained that the procedure would be painful and uncomfortable for both of us, and—considering how close my due date was—that it would most likely induce an early delivery. Needless to say, this news didn't exactly line up with my Desire Factor in relation to the birth of my son.

When I got home from that doctor's appointment, I relaxed my body and mind. I let go of all the facts I had just been given, breathed away the feelings of anxiety and tension that my imaginings had stirred within me, and allowed myself to sink back into the knowledge that the manifestation of everything I desire is only about an alignment of energy. I breathed deeply and connected with my heartfelt desire: to usher this beautiful being safely, joyously, and easily into the world. Going deeper, I allowed myself to experience the richness of the connection that I already felt between Maxim and me. I remembered all the times he had kicked in direct response to something I had been thinking, remembering, or feeling. I allowed myself to feel the incredible blessing of sharing a physical body with another soul. I felt deep appreciation for his brilliance, his intelligence, his sensitivity to me, and my sensitivity to him.

In this heightened state of meditation and appreciation, I connected with Maxim soul to soul and telepathically showed him the situation that my doctor had just presented to me. Softly, I explained that we could do this the hard way, with the doctor manually attempting to shift his body from the outside—and I offered him an image of what that might look and feel like—or we could do it the easy way. I lovingly transmitted a picture of him effortlessly repositioning himself so he was head down in the birth canal.

As I imagined this scenario unfolding, I actually began to expect that he would choose the second option, because it was, after all, the most logical, comfortable, and natural position for him to be in. Continuing to feel the immensity of love I have for this child, I imagined and expected that of course he would move and we would not have to go through with the procedure. That night, I went into labor, and when we arrived at the hospital, the doctor confirmed that he was head down and ready to go. It was the easiest delivery I could have imagined.

Manifestations like these—which some might even label as miraculous—are not miracles at all. Nor are they a function of luck, of coincidence, of good karma, or of destiny or fate. They are the result of systematically retraining ourselves to stay attuned to our own energy so we can receive the early, subtle clues sent to us by our emotional guidance system and then make adjustments as needed. Learning to redirect our focus within so we can reclaim our power over our energy is a skill that has to be developed, one that requires continued practice, because it flies in the face of how most of us were taught to relate to the world. But this is the only way we can develop awareness as to when something feels right and choose to take that action—and know when something feels wrong

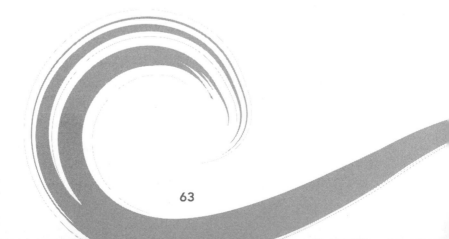

and choose not to take the action. Only by tuning in to our own energy are we able to recognize the path that will align us with our Desire Factor.

The more in tune we become with our own energy fields, the more we're able to guide our thoughts and feelings along a course of positive, rather than negative, expectation. And like any new habit, with enough practice, it soon becomes second nature. We carry with us the knowledge that of course we're fabulous, of course we're important, and of course the things we desire fall easily and joyfully into place. And when things aren't turning out the way we'd like in some particular moment and we lose our balance, we know how to regain it—not by demanding others to change but by making the energetic adjustment within ourselves.

Chapter 3: The Principle of Joyful Expectancy— Applying It Step by Step

1   When you think about the object, condition, or experience that is currently igniting your Desire Factor, do you typically feel good or bad?

2   What are your beliefs about your Desire Factor? Do you believe you are well on your way to reaching your goal or that success will be difficult or impossible to achieve? Notice whether your beliefs about your desire feel good or bad.

3 How would you like to feel about your Desire Factor?

4 What beliefs would you have to cultivate in order to relate to your desire in a way that excites and inspires you?

5 Raise the frequency of your dominant thoughts and beliefs to the vibration of joyful expectancy. Use the following process to assist you in this.

Energy Mastery Exercise

Generating Joyful Magnetism

Begin by finding a comfortable, quiet place to be and gently close your eyes. Take a nice deep breath in, and let it out. And with each inhale, imagine you're opening up more and more to the broader part of you, to your divine counterpart.

Take another deep breath in, and as you do, imagine bringing even more of the nonphysical, spiritual essence that is you into your physical body. And as you breathe out, just imagine that any thoughts you don't want, any energy that doesn't serve you, is leaving your physical body. Each time you breathe in, imagine that you're breathing in a high, refined energy—the energy of the vast, nonphysical entity that you are.

Imagine that your inner being—the essence and spirit within you that animates your mind and body, that allows your heart to beat, that literally breathes life force into you and through you—is becoming the focal point of your awareness. With every breath, allow yourself to feel more of that life force, more of that well-being, more of the creator that you truly are, flowing through and around your physical body.

Notice that the more attention you give to your inner being, the more you are filled with pure positive energy. Just take a moment to feel that connection. This connection—this love—is always flowing to you, through you, and around you as unlimited possibility and potential. You are both a creator and a receiver of this love.

And now call into your awareness something that you deeply desire—a reality that you want to experience that you haven't yet experienced in all its fullness. It could be a more steady or abundant stream of money. It could be an exciting new relationship. It could be an increase in your number of projects or clients. Just allow yourself to identify one thing that is right now igniting the Desire Factor within you, and acknowledge the strength and the potency of this desire.

And now, very deliberately, call on the power of your focus to bring to mind all of the reasons why you are now closer to fulfilling this desire than you've ever been before. You might say things to yourself such as, "I now have more clarity about what I really want and why. I have more tools available to me in this moment than at any other time in my life. I am understanding more and more about how manifestations occur, and I am becoming more masterful at directing my energy." Deliberately advocate for your own success by bringing to mind all of the evidence that already points to it.

And with another breath, allow yourself to visualize a white screen in your mind with the most dominant beliefs you hold in relation to this desire written across it. As you read each one, notice how it feels. If it is a belief that feels good and you want to keep it, imagine surrounding it with light and energizing it even more. If it's a belief that feels bad and you want to change it, imagine erasing it from the white screen and writing in its place a statement of how you intend to feel instead.

And now, taking another deep breath, consciously invite into yourself the sensation of what joyful anticipation feels like to you. Think back to a time when you felt eager, positive expectation, and allow that feeling to manifest as a physical sensation. How does joyful eagerness feel in your physical body? Breathe into that feeling for a few minutes, allowing it to expand.

Taking another light-filled breath, say to yourself either silently or out loud: "I now draw to me all things that are for my higher good. I am magnetic to success, and success is magnetized toward me." Feel all manner of good things coming into your vibrational experience. Your only work is to receive. As your light shines brightly, pulsating outward, it is simultaneously bringing more light in. The more light you can hold, the more success, abundance, and prosperity flows into your experience.

Take a moment to receive the benefits of this energy work that you just accomplished and to allow your improved point of attraction to settle into you in a very positive, pleasurable way. Thank yourself for being open and for receiving more of who you are. And when you are ready, begin to slowly wiggle your fingers and toes . . . sense the room you are sitting in . . . feel the sensation of your body being supported by the chair . . . and slowly open your eyes.

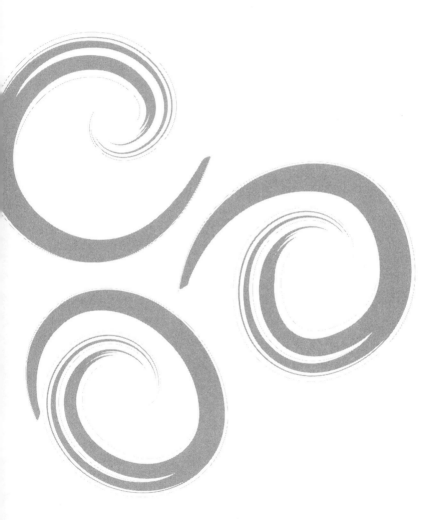

4

The Principle of Having

*To have is to hold. When you consistently have the energetic
experience of having what you desire, without split energy, you
will have your desire. You are in a vibrational universe, and the
experience of having brings the fulfillment of the desire.
You will never have what you feel is lacking. Ever.*

The Quantum Council

As you of course know by now, this is a book about deliberate creation, about guiding you in the manifestation of
anything you desire—not through old-school practices like goal setting, visualizing, and repeating affirmations, but through mastering
the energies that orchestrate and manage every act of creation, big or
small. And since this mastery does require a working understanding
of universal law, I'd like to take a moment to dispel a very com
mon misperception shared by many people whose first introduction
to Law of Attraction came via watching or reading *The Secret*. It's
vital that you understand that the process of manifestation is not as

one-dimensional as simply thinking about what you desire and having it magically materialize before your eyes. We cannot just think our desires into being, and to expect that we can is to negate the powerful realm of energy which is the birthplace of all creation.

As we've already explored, your thoughts are extremely powerful, inasmuch as they generate a vibrational frequency that is broadcasted far and wide. The universe responds to the vibration you are broadcasting, and this vibration is made known to you through the precise guidance system of your moment-by-moment moods and emotions. *The Secret* was helpful in the sense that it provided at least the basic understanding that each of us is the creator of our own life experience. And yet, over the years, I've worked with countless people who had become frustrated, angry, and even more deeply resigned when trying to implement its concepts, because the picture it painted of how manifestation works was incomplete.

See, what's missing from most explanations of deliberate creation is the understanding that because this universe operates solely under the principles of inclusion and attraction, we draw to ourselves more of whatever vibration we're offering—whether that vibration is one of sufficiency and abundance or one of lack and discontent. So, for example, if you're asking for something from a perception of yearning for it, lacking it, or needing it, such as "I need more money," "I need a better job," or "I need to save my marriage or find my true love," it's the vibration of *need* that the universe hears and responds to, not your ultimate goal of manifesting the money, the career, or the love.

And so, if your vibration around money is that you want or need more of it, Law of Attraction will add momentum to your experience of wanting and needing more money. Whatever you ask for, the universe only has one answer, and that answer is yes. It gives you more of whatever vibration is active within you when you ask. So the sentiment "I really, really want _____" (whether you give words to it or not) conveys exactly the same message energetically as "I am really, really lacking _____."

A lonely person cannot simply think their soul mate into existence. You can't get to an experience of love or connection when the vibration you're offering is one of feeling heartbroken or abandoned. Likewise, you can't get to financial solvency from an emotional stance of feeling broke. When the signal we're sending to the universe is one of desperation rather than satisfaction, we render ourselves about as receptive as a Teflon frying pan, skillfully deflecting all of the amazing experiences that are seeking to adhere themselves to our lives.

The vibration of wanting is laden with resistance, angst, and yearning. When we desire something to the point of feeling we need it to happen, we introduce stress, anxiety, and desperation into the equation, which makes it far more difficult for what we want to make its way into our experience. If you've ever been approached by a guy who was really yearning for the attention of a woman, or interviewed someone who desperately needed the job, you know that the vibration of desperation is palpable—and utterly repulsive from an energy standpoint. In our state of neediness, we actually push away and scare the very people and things we desire. And so, as you consider your heartfelt desire, you want to begin to notice which vibration has the strongest momentum within you— is it the vibration of wanting it or the vibration of right now, in this moment, having it?

The moment you accept your desire as a possibility—when you acknowledge its presence and allow its energy to move through you—that desire actually becomes a part of your consciousness. You already "have" it, even though it is still in an invisible form. By embracing rather than repressing or denying your desire, you shift from a state of neediness to a state of fulfillment. This is the essence of the Principle of Having.

There are only two fundamental stances, attitudes, or perspectives that we can hold in relation to anything we desire: One is the vibration of wanting (or needing) it. And the other is the vibration of already having it. If we can tip that vibrational fulcrum from wanting to having, by even as slight a margin as one degree, we speed the rate of our manifestations exponentially. And that's exactly what we're going to explore in this chapter.

To Have or Have Not

The vibrational state of wanting, yearning, or needing is created out of a perception that what we desire is somehow separate from us— either in time, space, or consciousness. And the vibrational state of having, on the other hand, comes from the experience of being in complete alignment with what we desire. Once we understand through the Principle of Alignment that we are already one with our source, which is the infinite supply of everything we could possibly desire, we can then begin to attune to the feeling of already having.

I started thinking the other day about all of the different contexts in which we use the word *have*, so I decided to look up the origins of the word. It turns out, it's a derivative of the Old English word *habban*, which means, "to own, possess; be subject to, or experience." I agree completely with this definition, especially when we apply it to the subtle realm of energy.

The big misconception about the idea of having is that it's something we'll experience somewhere out in the future, once we've made our way to our goal. This thought process goes something like this: *I don't yet have what I desire, so therefore I desire it, and once I get it, I'll have it.* This places our happiness out in the future, accessible to us only after we've attained the result or manifested the outcome, and it completely strips us of our power in the present. The mind-set that once we achieve the goal or fulfill the desire, we'll finally be happy is the cause of so much human suffering. And this notion is absolutely rampant in our culture. We say things to one another like, "*Have* a good time at the party!"—as though the joyful having we're wishing for that person exists anywhere outside of themselves! As though the experience of having a good time or a joyful time or an interesting time is something that can be hunted down, captured, and held forever in our pockets. The notion that *having* is a future destination, or something elusive that we must search the world to find, is wholly and completely vibrationally inaccurate.

A broader understanding of the word *having* unfolds when we consider its vibrational application. Because whatever you desire to have—whether it's a good time at the party or a gorgeous home on the hill, a fit and flexible body, or a passionate and supportive marriage—you'll be going about it the hard way if you're seeking to "get" it from somewhere out there. It's this approach to fulfilling desires that has people chasing the next fad diet, online dating site, and get-rich-quick scheme. The much easier way to obtain anything you desire is by acknowledging that, energetically speaking, you already *have* it, because you are it.

Having exists right here, right now. The moment you conceived the desire, it was yours. You *had* it in consciousness, and consciousness is the birthplace of all things. You received the desire. It is now yours. You are literally *having* the experience of that desire, in whatever state of becoming it's currently in. The moment you accept that desire—when you contemplate it, accept it, own it, and feel the energy of it building inside of you—it's yours, long before there is any physical or tangible evidence of its existence. You know that what you desire already exists, because you can feel the presence of it within you.

The Bible tells us that "faith is the substance of things hoped for, the evidence of things not yet seen." Faith is the secret ingredient demonstrated by powerful, magnetic leaders across all ages and walks of life. Their conviction that what they desire is in the process of coming to pass is so compelling that it inspires even the most skeptical into action. True leaders stand firm in the Principle of Having, even as the object of their desire is still invisible to the masses. Now that's power! The vibration of having is incredibly attractive. It communicates the self-confidence that makes us want to flock to those who convey it, and they to us.

So at one end of the Desire Factor spectrum we have the experience of yearning, needing, and wanting—the experience of lack. And at the other end, we have the experience of joy for having given birth to the desire in the first place, the faith in its eventual becoming, and the certainty that because the seed of the desire has been planted within us, it's just a matter of achieving the right season and climate and it will bloom fully. On the having end of the continuum, we acknowledge the abundant nature of the source that created us, and we have no doubt in its ability to nourish any dream to full fruition.

Remember that in every moment we have access to every nuance of energy that exists anywhere in the universe. We have access to the energy of joy. We have access to the energy of love. We have access to the energy of empowerment, of certainty, of clarity, of freedom. We have unlimited access to all of these experiences and more, because the access point to all of these frequencies is within us. Once we break our desire down into its essential energetic components, well-being, abundance, success, creativity, loving and supportive relationships, and anything else we might desire are ours for the taking.

Breaking Down Your Desire

When you break any desire down into its most basic energetic components, you'll begin to see that those components are available to you right now. You do not need to wait until the actual desire has been manifested before you begin residing in that energy. And the more you allow yourself to bask in the energy of having it in this present moment, the faster your life experience will morph into the configuration you desire. I recently guided my friend Jordon, who had been trying unsuccessfully for over a year to lose weight, through the process of breaking down her desire.

I first asked her to state her desire as clearly as she was able to articulate it from her present vantage point. She wrote, "I desire to have a fit, flexible, good-looking, good-feeling body." Pretty clear, right? I then asked her to break this desire down into its most basic energetic components. In other words, if she was already living in her fit, flexible, good-looking, good-feeling body, what would she experience that she's not experiencing now? How would she feel? What qualities or latent characteristics did she believe would become available to her as a result of having achieved this manifestation? Jordon easily came up with a list of qualities that she associated with creating her ideal body. Self-confidence. Efficiency. Endurance. Pride. And then she landed upon the vibration that held the most significance to her. She said, "Freedom."

Jordon associated the manifestation of her ideal body with the vibration of having freedom in its many forms: Freedom of movement. Freedom of self-expression. The freedom to be comfortable in her body and to wear whatever she wanted to wear without angst. With this part of the exercise, we had penetrated her surface desires and gotten to the essence of what she was really seeking through her desire to lose weight.

Now that we had uncovered that the essential feeling of freedom was what she was seeking, I guided her to begin nibbling away (so to speak!) at the notion of freedom so she could begin to acknowledge and build on the areas in her life where she already feels free. I asked her, "Where in your life do you have an abundance of freedom of self-expression?" Her answer came easily. "I have total freedom of self-expression in my work. I have freedom when I sing. I have the freedom to decorate and organize my home in any way I want to. Also, my children are grown," she went on. "I'm free to make dinner or not make dinner, to stock the house full of groceries or to buy a very limited range of foods. I can go to the gym anytime day or night. In fact, I can come and go anywhere I like, as I please." With this simple step, Jordon began shifting her energy from feeling constricted from carrying the extra weight, to tapping into a feeling of complete freedom in many aspects of her life.

Lastly, I asked Jordon to consider where in her life she could expand and enhance her experience of free self-expression. In other words, how could she take the freedom she was already experiencing and build on it? Again, she quickly saw areas where she could accentuate her experience of already having the freedom that represents the essence of her desire. "I could do a better job of expressing the things I enjoy and desire to my boyfriend," she said. "I could join a hiking group that travels to places that interest me. I could sign up for that yoga retreat I've been thinking about doing. I could allow myself to dress for complete comfort and self-expression when I am on my own time." I left Jordon with the assignment to continue expanding her experience of freedom in all of the ways she had already identified, and in all the ways that would continue to come to her in the weeks and months to come. And most importantly, I reminded her that the feeling of freedom she formerly believed she would only have once she lost twenty pounds is available to her now, and I encouraged her to celebrate it every time she experienced it in the moment.

See, the illusion is that we have to make the change or get the thing or achieve the result and then we'll experience the feelings we've assigned to that particular outcome or destination. But this is entirely out of sync with the laws of the universe. The way it really works is this: First we conjure the feeling, and then circumstances assemble themselves around that energy. You do not need to wait until the result is accomplished before you experience the essence of having your desire. You don't even need to attach the feeling to that specific desire. You can look for the feeling and acknowledge it everywhere it shows itself to you, and the more you look for it, the more evidence of it you will find all around you.

Maybe you have had the experience of being so committed to the successful manifestation of something, because it really mattered to you a lot, that you were unfazed by doubt, judgment, or criticism—whether it was being offered to you from others or from yourself. You were so purely and powerfully acting as if what you wanted was a foregone conclusion that you were unwilling to even consider any other scenario. At some deep level of personal resolution within yourself, perhaps you sensed that you simply could not afford to give one ounce of airtime to considering any outcome that opposed your desire, so you just. didn't. let. yourself. go. there. Instead, you remained steadfast, your eyes fixated on the prize, and all of your mental, emotional, and spiritual energy being channeled power-fully in that same direction, with no siphon in the hose. This is the Principle of Having.

Making the shift from wanting to having means generating 100 percent solidarity with the fulfillment of your desire and carry-ing that resolve with you everywhere you go, even when no one else around you can see it. I experienced this when my son Maxim had to have a long and often painful series of procedures, includ-ing open-heart surgery, when he was just two months of age. Even though the optics of his tiny body being poked and prodded were excruciating, even though we encountered everything from igno-rant comments made by family members to terrifying prognoses set forth by medical staff, Frederic and I remained absolutely steadfast in the having of our heartfelt desire. We were walking out of that hospital with our healthy and happy baby in our arms, period.

Situations like these, where we find ourselves face-to-face with a condition that completely opposes something we powerfully desire, are the hardest to apply the Principle of Having. It's incredibly difficult to relax into the knowledge of absolute well-being in the face of a frightening diagnosis. It's hard to remain connected to the energy of having plenty of money in the bank when you're unemployed or up against a mountain of debt. And it's not easy to reside in the energy of harmony and connection with someone you love when your relationship is in the midst of turmoil. The "reality" of these situations simply feels too big, too compelling, and we may even feel that we're being irresponsible if we don't face them fully. But in terms of your mastery of deliberate creation, this is precisely what is required. It's in those exact moments when "what is" is in greatest defiance to the Desire Factor within us that we must summon the full power of our focus. We simply must conjure—from memory, from imagination, or from deliberately exposing ourselves to the personal triumphs of others—the vibration of what we want and give ourselves permission to leave behind the vibration of what we currently have.

We have to first start with the understanding that whatever the current circumstance, it was created first in consciousness—and that consciousness is never static but is always in a state of evolution. We have to remind ourselves that nothing in this world is permanent, even ill health or debt. Everything is being created in each new, now moment. What has already manifested is not easy to ignore: after all, it's loud, it's bold, and it's up close and personal in living color in our life experience. But if we continue to give the majority of our attention to what currently is, we will continue to re-create that experience. To create a different outcome, we must find a way to get into the having mode of what we do want. Once we've made the shift in energy, the circumstances will begin to turn around.

And so, if you have a condition that you're clear you do not want to persist in your experience, such as financial debt when you desire financial prosperity, for example, there are of course some logical courses of action that you can take. You do need to continue to pay the bills, and you do need to continue looking for solutions to earn the money you require. The trick is to take those actions while still generating within yourself the energy of having the abundance you desire. Now, this does not mean spending money you don't have. It means taking the action journey of continuing to pay down your debt while simultaneously bringing yourself vibrationally into alignment with the feelings of freedom, security, and joy of having your credit cards at a zero balance and an all-sufficiency of money in your bank account. Remember that the vast majority of every manifestation occurs in the invisible realm of energy before it is tangible enough to be seen. The secret to being a masterful deliberate creator is to keep our attention on what is in the process of becoming, knowing that it's just a matter of time until it will be realized fully in the realm of form.

It was a full month from the time that Maxim's heart condition was first diagnosed to the day when the final procedure was completed, but because we remained in the vibration of having and didn't allow ourselves to dip into the frequency of wanting, yearning, or pleading—the experience of Maxim's hospitalization remains one of the most powerful testaments of the accuracy of the laws of the universe, and my own ability to cooperate with them, that I have experienced to date.

Our experience with Maxim's full recovery is neither unusual nor uncommon. In fact, stories just like it abound. One night in 1985, when actor Jim Carrey was a young Los Angeles comic struggling just to make ends meet, he drove his beat-up Toyota to the top of Mulholland Drive. Sitting there, broke, looking down over the opulence of the city and dreaming of the house he would one day live in and the car he would one day drive, he followed an impulse. He pulled out his checkbook and wrote himself a check for ten million dollars, writing in the notation line, "For acting services rendered," and dated it ten years in the future, payable on Thanksgiving of 1995.

Exactly ten years later, just before Thanksgiving 1995, after starring in wildly successful box-office hit movies like *Ace Ventura: Pet Detective*, *The Mask*, and *Liar Liar*, Jim landed the lead role in his fourth film that year, *Dumb and Dumber*. His fee for the movie? Yep. A cool ten million dollars. A true deliberate creator, Carrey didn't wait to get the big role or the big payday to start feeling that he *had* the success he desired. He felt the *having* of the success, and the big roles—and the big money—found him. And that's just the way it always works, whether you're talking about the manifestation of abundance or success or love. You have to find the feeling first, and the circumstances will morph around it. When you're committed to the Principle of Having, you look for any little piece of evidence that supports the successful unfolding of your desire, and you invest all of your attention and energy in fanning the flame of it. Slowly but surely, the fulcrum begins to tip and the up-swinging momentum takes on a life of its own.

My girlfriend Shannon did this—albeit unknowingly—during her high-risk pregnancy, when doctors had given her identical twins only a 40 percent chance of survival. Strangulation caused by umbilical cord compression was the biggest risk, and in fact, multiple ultrasounds revealed there were already eight true knots in her babies' umbilical cords. Unwilling to allow the possibility of giving birth to deceased babies to persist for even a moment, Shannon logged dozens of hours at the local university's medical library researching articles and medical protocol, and one day she hit upon a discovery that tipped the momentum of her pregnancy from that moment forward. Wharton's jelly, she learned, is a naturally occurring substance produced during pregnancy for the exact purpose of lubricating and strengthening the umbilical cord, thus protecting the baby against cord compression or strangulation.

Shannon locked onto this discovery like a dog on a bone. She visualized the presence of this substance—thick and nourishing—surrounding, lubricating, and protecting her babies' umbilical cords. She thought about the brilliance of the human body to naturally produce whatever is needed to support the development of a growing fetus and to ensure the baby's safe passage. And she acknowledged and gave thanks for the brilliance of her unborn daughters, and appreciated them both silently and out loud for their ability to adapt and thrive in their unique situation. Shannon used her discovery of Wharton's jelly as a reason to focus on the *having* she desired, not on the *having* she feared, and this one discovery set the tone for the remainder of her pregnancy. Not only did she realize her intended outcome of delivering healthy baby girls, but she also saved herself the unbearable grief of thinking, feeling, and imagining in opposition to this heartfelt desire.

The Principle of Having prepares you internally to be ready to receive the external manifestation of your desire. It is the principle of acting as if—of building it, as the saying goes, because you know that they will come. It's practicing the vibration of your lover before you meet. It's clearing your calendar to be able to take the trip before any travel plans are on the books. It's adjusting your mind-set to embrace that higher tax bracket even before you actually receive the promotion. Having is leaning in to what's vibrationally in the process of becoming, because you know that once you've invested your powerful creative energy into that outcome, the universe simply must provide it.

To make the jump from needing to having, you have to take a leap of faith—not with your actions but with your vibration. Rather than being your typical skeptical self and dipping one toe in the water, so to speak, you have to commit yourself fully to the swim. You just can't live a masterful life while sitting on the edge of the river, because everything you want is downstream from where you are. If you really come to know this, if you allow yourself to believe and make yourself pliable through nonresistance, the current will simply carry you. If you can embody these subtle vibrational changes, if you can integrate the frequency of already *having* your desire as a natural part of your personality, if you can walk and talk and think and show up as the person who has created that which you desire in the potent inner world of vibration, you will have made the shift from wanting to having, and a different reality will begin to coalesce around your new energetic stance. It really is as simple as that.

You are the attractor of your life's experiences. You are the one who mines the gold—or the scrap metal—from the infinite resources of this universe. You are the miner, and you are mining for the treasure chest filled with your unique desires, for what you have identified as your version of gold. The Principle of Having is the principle of mining. But you are not mining for something that exists out there as some faraway destination you have to make your way to. You are mining for the realization of your desires in each new

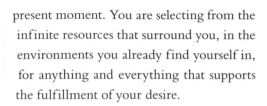

present moment. You are selecting from the infinite resources that surround you, in the environments you already find yourself in, for anything and everything that supports the fulfillment of your desire.

You mine for the treasures of your desire through the power of your focus and through the strength of your commitment. You mine for it by deliberately focusing upon what it is you want to see rather than its absence. You mine for your desire by acknowledging that you already have a piece of it. It's already yours, by virtue of the fact that you desire it. The moment that desire was born within you, the moment it arose within your heart, your vibrational signature was inextricably tied to it. You and your desire are one. It exists within you, now, in this present moment. The desire itself is the thread that connects you to every future experience you want to unfold.

Each desire that is born within you is like a potent seed. Like a kernel of corn or a watermelon seed, our desires are encoded with all the intelligence they need to grow into their full, unique expressions. In other words, each desire is ripe with the infinite possibilities of the universe at large. But it's our personal vibration—indicated by our moment-by-moment emotion—that provides the nourishment that allows the idea of our desires to sprout, grow, and blossom into all that they can become. It is the daily mood or vibrational stance that we offer toward that which we desire that determines whether it manifests or dies on the vine.

Desire in its purest form is not attached to need, nor to lack of any kind. Desire is the mechanism of expansion, the engine that drives our never-ending state of becoming. There is pure joy in desire. Without it, life is empty, flavorless, meaningless, and without passion. To return to the natural joyful state of eagerly anticipating something wanted, which most of us knew as children, we simply have to purify our desires. When we separate out the vibrations of need and yearning that drag our desires down, what remains is the very essence of what life has called us, in this new moment, to ask for. To achieve purity of desire, we not only need to make peace with the fact that there will always be something we've asked for that we haven't yet received—we must also fall in love with the unmanifested desire itself.

Chapter 4: The Principle of Having— Applying It Step by Step

1. In relation to your current Desire Factor, notice whether you are typically more focused on the presence of your evolving desire or on the absence of its manifestation. Which do you experience more often: the feeling of yearning or the feeling of having?

2. What evidence is available to you right now that would support and enhance your experience of already having that which you desire? For example, if you desire greater financial security, you could use as a focal point the feeling of security that you already experience in other aspects of your life. If you desire to fall back into love or restore intimacy in an important relationship, what other sources of love and intimacy could you focus on and therefore allow to expand?

3   Discover the thoughts, actions, and daily practices that can serve you in shifting your focus from wanting to already having. The following experiential exercise will support you in this.

Energy Mastery Exercise

Accepting the Presence of That Which You Desire

*B*egin by closing your eyes and taking a few slow, deep breaths. And as you breathe, feel the sensation of your ribs and chest expanding. Allow your inhale to really nourish you, to bring you more fully into this moment, more fully connected with yourself. And with your exhale, just allow yourself to release anything you're holding on to—any stress from your day, any thoughts about the future, even any expectations about this process. Just imagine all of that rolling down your body with gravity, through your feet, and into the ground beneath you. Give yourself permission to experience a shift in perspective on the subject of one of your deeply held, heartfelt desires.

And now, again bring to mind your unique Desire Factor, the particular object or condition that you have identified as something you want. And recall once again the feelings you believe you will experience once this desire has been fulfilled. Is it a feeling of pride? A feeling of joy? A feeling of lightness? A feeling of increased self-confidence or empowerment that permeates all aspects of your experience? Breathe into these feelings, allowing the essence of them to seep into all dimensions of you—body, mind, and heart.

Feel the shift in your personal vibration as you deliberately conjure and invite into your being the essence of your desire.

And with another deep breath, acknowledge that the origin of these feelings—and every other feeling—comes from within you. No one can assert a feeling into your experience, and your feelings are not the byproduct of an external manifestation. The feelings you associate with the manifestation of your desire—whether they are feelings of pride or lightness or empowerment—exist as a frequency that you have the power to tune in to from within yourself. And through the power of your focus, you can expand your experience of oneness with the object of your desire, right here and right now.

Give yourself permission to attune your frequency to the fulfillment of your Desire Factor and to make room for all that it will bring into your life. Say to yourself, "With my mind, heart, and soul, I accept the fulfillment of this desire now." Feel the energy that represents the fulfillment of your desire entering into your being and upgrading your consciousness. Take a moment to appreciate how good it feels to allow this higher vibration to pulsate through you.

Acknowledge that the moment this desire was born within you, you entered into a relationship with it, and as a result, your desire and you became one. Say to yourself, "Because I have accepted the fulfillment of my desire, I now have it. I now have the object of my desire. I no longer need what I formerly desired, because I now have it! Through this knowledge, I know that I already *am* that which I desire."

And with another breath, allow yourself to formulate an affirmation that acknowledges your present-moment connection with your Desire Factor. Begin this affirmation with the powerful words, "I am, " and then complete it by affirming the reality that is already in the process of coming into being. For example, "I *am* abundant," "I *am* successful," "I *am* a mom," "I *am* in a fulfilling relationship with my ideal partner."

Imagine a blank screen in your mind's eye, and play a mental movie of you already having the fulfillment of your desire. See yourself doing, being, having, and enjoying your desire with an overflowing feeling of gratitude and celebration. As you picture this scene, feel yourself being joyous, happy, loving, and free. Add color, sound, and dimension to the image, allowing it to come more fully to life.

Focus on every detail in your awareness, acknowledging that everything you are seeing, hearing, doing, and feeling is happening right now, in this present moment, and not at some distant point in the future. Feel the excitement of your desire already being fulfilled. See it! Feel it! Know it! And when you are ready, gently open your eyes.

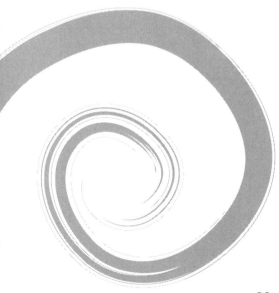

5

The Principle of Loving

The pure energy of love is what created you, the stars, the oceans, and the world. Love is the creative force in the universe that is a direct action from the Divine to bring creation into form. And because you are an extension of the Divine, and because you are a creator, your desires are also fueled by love.

The Quantum Council

*L*ove is an incredibly powerful force. It's the stuff that, as the poets say, makes the world go 'round. Love is the fuel that drives every act of creation—not by effort or coercion but through pure, unadulterated magnetic attraction. When we are attuned to the frequency of love, we easily rise above negativity, disbelief, and drama and become—at least in the moment of our alignment with it—completely immune to the doubts or negative opinions of others. Rather, we serve as our own source of certainty and stability. Love binds us to the object of our desire and helps us to remain steadfast and devoted to it, even in the presence of others who may have differing or opposing intentions. Loving generates within us a center of calm and knowing that helps us to navigate the chaos of the world, and which continually brings us back to what is important. Love transmutes all lower frequencies.

Love places the lover and the object of love in the same vibrational location. When we love, we close time and space. There is no separation between who we hope to be and who we already are. Loving can transcend all boundaries, obstacles, and social constructs. It is the force that draws strangers together from across a room. It's what makes every good cause worth fighting for. Love is the highest vibration that anyone can achieve, and it is the key to fulfilling every desire.

The Principle of Having taught us that our desires exist, right now, in vibrational form. The Principle of Loving teaches us that we already have a relationship with that desire, and by consciously, playfully, and lovingly flowing our energy toward it, we strengthen the quality of that relationship. Take a moment to really consider this: *you already have a relationship with your heartfelt desire.* This relationship was forged the moment the idea occurred to you for the very first time, and you have continued to evolve, expand, refine, and amend that desire ever since.

To really bring this concept home, I'd like you to conjure in your mind someone in your life who is extremely important to you—your child, for example, or a coworker or friend, or your spouse—someone with whom you currently have some type of relationship. What you will discover is that you actually carry a piece of this person's energy with you wherever you go. Your internal relationship with them exists—regardless of if you're sitting in the same room or if you're thousands of miles away. And the reason your connection with this person is so strong is due to all of the time, attention, intention, and energy you have invested in your relationship with them. You've nourished this connection with your attention and energy; you've spent time contemplating your relationship with them even when you are apart; you've imagined your future together; you've recalled positive feelings that you've shared together in the past and anticipated more positive experiences in the future. And all of this has created the relationship you now have with this person, whatever the state of that relationship might currently be.

Now, turn your attention to the quality of the relationship you currently have with your heartfelt desire. When you contemplate it, does it feel pure and exciting? Do you light up when you think about it? Are you loving the way it continues to evolve and expand, and loving the ways that life continues to show you why you want it? Or is your relationship with this precious desire burdened with doubt, with bad memories of past failures, or with disappointment that it hasn't yet been fully realized? And here's an even more important question to consider: Do you believe your desire *deserves* your loving attention, even if it's still in the process of becoming? To bridge the gap between where you are and where you want to be, your answer to this question must be a resounding, unequivocal yes.

In order for any relationship to grow, it must be fed and nourished. And the way you nourish your relationship with your desire is through your loving attention, imagination, and energy. Think about it this way: If you had a great first date with a man or woman who interests you, who inspires you, who lights you up, would you just leave that experience in the past and forget about it? No way, right?! You would rehash every delicious moment of it; you'd bore your friends by poring over every detail about it; you would imagine the possibilities and daydream about what might happen next. And you would love every step of the relationship's unfolding.

The experience of falling in love mirrors the process of creation itself. Like deliberate creation, falling in love demands a trust fall. Our heart simply leads the way—often without any conscious permission or decision on our part. And, rather than giving in to

doubt or insecurity, rather than withholding our love until the relationship has grown into an objective, tangible, concrete form, we simply allow ourselves to love, to imagine, to hope, to dream, and to believe—even though the relationship may still be in its infancy.

If your desire is to become a parent, would you withhold your love for the fetus in the womb just because he or she has not yet emerged as a fully developed baby? Do you withhold your love for the dream vacation you're planning just because you're still in the process of sorting out all of the details? Do you withhold your love—which is the same as saying your creativity and genius—from the meal you're preparing just because it isn't yet plated and ready to eat? Of course not! You love each step along the way of these experiences unfolding, knowing that they will of course culminate into the delicious three-dimensional realities that you can experience and enjoy with all of your physical senses.

This is exactly the kind of relationship you want to keep creating and strengthening with each of your desires. You want the energy and essence of that future reality to become so dominant within you that your present awareness has no choice but to harmonize with this energy and, as a result, magnetize more of it. As you already know, the moment you gave birth to that desire, it manifested in the realm of energy. It exists right now in a state of pure potentiality, which you can tap into at any moment. The only thing to do now is to consciously shorten the distance between you, and you do this through the Principle of Loving.

The Bridge between Loving and Lack

Let's return for a moment to the emotional continuum that we explored in chapter 3. At the high end of the spectrum, our emotional guidance system lets us know when our dominant vibration is one of abundance, possibility, certainty, empowerment, and ease. And how do we know that we're vibrating in resonance with abundance, possibility, certainty, empowerment, and ease? Because we feel absolutely amazing. We're on fire, in the zone, and moving with little to no resistance toward every outcome we desire. At the low end of that continuum, negative emotions like sadness, fear, discouragement, or frustration indicate that we are vibrating in the range of insufficiency, lack, and doubt, and are therefore in a state of resistance to our own desires.

The reality that unfolds in our experience depends entirely upon which end of this emotional continuum we are vibrating. Let's examine just a few of the different ways that life can occur to us when seen through the expansive perspective of appreciation versus when we are viewing it through the narrow lens of insufficiency:

- Seeing through the lens of appreciation vs. looking for evidence of lack

- Giving and receiving freely vs. not giving or being open to receive

- Opening your heart vs. closing your heart

- Expecting the best to happen vs. worrying that the worst will happen

- Coming from your heart vs. devolving into power struggles

- Acknowledging infinite possibilities vs. focusing on shortage

- Wanting everyone to succeed vs. competing with others

- Focusing on how you can serve others vs. thinking only of what others will give you

- Telling yourself why you can have what you desire vs. telling yourself why you can't

- Acting from your integrity vs. compromising your values or ideals

- Paying attention to universal clues as they unfold vs. operating on autopilot

- Applauding others' success vs. feeling threatened by it

Reviewing this list, it seems fairly obvious that the frequency of lack yields radically different results than the frequency of abundance. The question that now arises is, How can we move into a state of loving the abundance that is all around us when we perceive our current situation as one of lack?

Some version of this question has been posed by nearly every school of thought throughout the self-improvement movement, and each has offered different practices and techniques for shifting our internal state of being and cultivating a more positive mental attitude. The philosophy behind these techniques is solid, because as we change the set point of the habitual vibrations we are offering, everything in the manifest universe responds to and reflects this change. However, techniques like affirmation and visualization usually aren't powerful enough to reverse the direction of a downward emotional spiral and usually end up causing more frustration than relief.

All things that are in motion—including our thoughts and emotions—carry with them a certain degree of momentum, and our chronic moods and vibrational states are no different. In the midst of an uncomfortable emotional extreme such as disappointment, betrayal, or rage, we may turn to practices like affirmations and visualizations, hoping that like a magic wand they will guide us away from unwanted emotions and into more pleasurable ones. But when we understand our emotions as a highly refined guidance system that reflects back to us the state of being we're focused on within each moment, we begin to see that these types of quantum leaps in consciousness are often just not possible. We can't suddenly pivot from despair to joy, from hopelessness to confidence, or from lack to abundance on a dime. But if our aim is simply to return to a state of neutrality, we can gradually reverse unwanted momentum and turn the tides of our own vibration in a more favorable direction.

The Tipping Point

The turning points in our lives that we relish and adore—those moments when we can feel the wind begin to change and the fulcrum start to lean in our favor . . . when we see the first glimmer of hope that an unwanted situation has the potential of improving— these turning points are the natural consequence of deliberately looking for and finding the neutral, vibrational middle ground of sufficiency. We have no power to improve a situation that we're actively railing against. We first have to achieve a state of acceptance for a situation, acknowledgment of its positive aspects, and appreciation for the ways it is currently serving us before we can make any significant forward gain. We may not be able to find evidence of lavish prosperity in the midst of paralyzing debt, or conjure the feeling of love in the middle of a sharp pang of loneliness, but we can always find evidence of our own sufficiency if we are willing to look for it.

Whether it's a relationship that is no longer satisfying or a project that seems to have stalled out, the act of intentionally looking for what is sufficient, or good enough, about each person and situation is what creates within us the possibility for a turnaround. Our focus is powerful, and when we choose to deliberately fan the flame of each glimmer of hope by acknowledging all the positive and satisfying aspects of our lives as they exist in each present moment, that fire continues to grow and the transformation we're seeking is well underway.

The undeniable fact is that we live in a universe of unending abundance, where all the elements necessary for us to thrive have already been provided. That we have air to breathe, water to drink, and the sun to keep us warm are obvious (and hugely overlooked and underappreciated) proof of our sufficiency and our abundance. Once we acknowledge the sufficiency that is all around us, we are just a short step away—in emotional and vibrational terms—from the state of appreciation. And in appreciation, all things that we nourish with the powerful energy of our attention expand, appreciate, and become more. Gradually, as we give more focus to what is working and what is wanted, rather than to what isn't working or isn't wanted, the fulcrum tips and our desires come more quickly to fruition.

What You Appreciate, Appreciates

The word *appreciate* is so interesting in that it has two distinct definitions that can help us to understand its broader significance. In an everyday sense, *to appreciate* is defined as "to be thankful or show gratitude for." But ask an accountant or a venture capitalist the meaning of the word, and they'll tell you that *appreciation* is "an increase in the value of an asset over time." The fastest way to allow into your life more of what you desire—both in the form of the feeling essence that you're really after and in terms of the material possessions that you believe will deliver that feeling—is to make it a daily, moment-by-moment practice to appreciate what you already have. In our constant striving toward the proverbial top of the mountain, it's so easy to lose sight of how much terrain we've already covered, how far we've come in the process. To appreciate is to deliberately decide to stop, turn around, and with a sense of satisfaction and accomplishment, take in the broad view that is all around you rather than focus only on the next destination that lies ahead.

Look around your life as it exists right at this moment, and you are certain to discover countless realities that you are now living that were once nebulous "someday" goals. The house you are living in,

perhaps, the relationships you have with
the people in your life, or the career
expression you are now living are all
things that may have once existed
only as an idea or a far-out dream.
There are so many aspects of yourself and your life that are already going
amazingly well—and most of these sustain themselves with absolutely no effort on
your part. The fact that you have the time and ability to read this book, that you have a fine mind that is receptive
to and capable of processing this information, and that you are an
expanding being who desires greater mastery in your own life—all
of this is cause for appreciation. That you live in some proximity
to nature's beauty and were born with senses that allow you to
perceive it is huge cause for appreciation. That you are a unique
individual, here with a unique purpose—and that you are passion-
ately interested in your own process of self-discovery—is cause for
appreciation.

The energy of appreciation is one of the most attractive, magnetic, and powerful energies in all the universe. When we are
appreciated by another, we feel seen, safe, validated, and inspired
to do, be, and give even more. But the real gift of appreciation
unfolds not when others shower it upon us but when we flow it
toward them. In appreciating someone or something, we generate
this same level of high-frequency emotion within ourselves because
we cannot appreciate our surroundings without bathing ourselves in
their abundant energy. As Voltaire, the eighteenth-century French
writer, pointed out, "Appreciation is a wonderful thing: it makes
what is excellent in others belong to us as well."

So appreciate where you stand in this exact moment. Appreciate
all that has come before, which gave you greater clarity about what

you now want. Appreciate all that you have learned and all that you have already manifested. Remember that you already have a relationship with every single one of your desires, and this relationship exists in the present moment, not somewhere out there in the future. And the maintenance of this relationship is something you must attend to continually, because as the saying goes, all things must grow or they die. The relationship with your ideal body is one that you want to nourish and attend to; so is the relationship with your children, your friends, your coworkers, and your significant other. In the same way, you have a relationship with all of the beautiful material possessions you have already manifested and acquired, and your active appreciation of them is what will keep those things alive and thriving in your experience.

As an example, I fell in love with my car the day I bought it—so much so that I have purchased the exact same make and model twice over the past several years. But my love and appreciation for that gorgeous machine is something that I allow myself to feel every time I get behind the wheel. The smell of the leather, the power of the engine, the smoothness of the ride, all of the places my car allows me to go with comfort and style and speed . . . I appreciate these things on the daily.

Dressing Yourself Up in Love

If you've ever fallen in love, you've experienced how love's powerful, happy, lighthearted energy seems to glow from your every pore. When you're in love, the whole world looks different. Everything seems possible, as if you are floating on a bubble that can carry you anywhere you want to go. The object of your love is all you want to talk about; it's all you want to think about. The high, expansive feeling of love bursts from your heart even before your eyes open in the morning, setting an energetic tone for your entire day. Creativity, energy, brilliance, and ideas that were once dormant now rush to the surface of your mind, imploring you into action. And the life-giving inspiration made available by the energy of love is not just limited to this one aspect of life. Far from it, actually. The energy of love might fuel you with the determination to finally take on that household project you've been avoiding. It may fill you with newfound clarity about what's important and which direction to go. The energy of loving reprioritizes all other aspects of your life into their proper place. Love carves the path and leads the way.

Think about the thoughts, emotions, and actions that come most easily when you've manifested a relationship with someone you love. You naturally flow positive energy in the direction of that person's well-being. You spend time envisioning the happy outcomes you desire—both for them as an individual and for your relationship together. You take actions with the intent of enhancing and contributing to their experience. You lean in the direction of happiness, and in the direction of sufficiency, acceptance, and satisfaction. You would never knowingly diminish the other person; rather, you take every opportunity to build them up. In other words, you do everything you can to keep the odds up that the relationship will succeed. And because you're intentionally looking for and finding their most positive aspects, you continue to attract more evidence of them. This becomes a self-perpetuating, self-replenishing cycle.

Every manifestation is in a state of constant becoming, which means it depends on our continued positive focus upon it in order to thrive. One of the most pervasive illusions of our human three-dimensional reality that we have to overcome is our perception that we ever "have" anything. In truth, we draw things into and out of our experience by virtue of our focus upon them. We draw them into and out of our experience by virtue of how much loving energy we flow to them. Your relationship with everything and everyone in your life must continue to evolve, and you are the one who focuses that next evolution into being. If there are manifestations in your life that you wish to revive, reconstitute, or completely deconstruct and reinvent, know for sure that you can accomplish this. And the way to do it is not by making an inventory of all its shortcomings but by enhancing and expanding on the aspects of it that you already love.

The joy you derive from any manifestation does not come from that person, place, or thing. The joy you feel is the joy that you yourself flow into that manifestation, which is then returned to you energetically. You are the originator of it all. In order to continue re-creating all the things we already love and appreciate about our lives, we must allow our consciousness to evolve from the Principle of Having to the Principle of Loving. If we stop only at the having, we'll stifle the further evolution and expansion of our desires. This is why it's so important not to become complacent about the things you have already manifested. Continue to use them as objects of attention to which you can flow your energy and your love. That is the secret for attracting more, and for making old things fresh and new.

Hold your desire close to you. Court it with your loving attention. Take it with you wherever you go. As you get in your car on your way to a work-related event, mentally affirm to yourself,

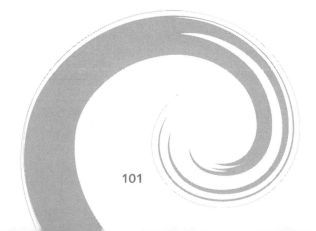

"This is me and my millions of dollars on our way to this event." As you're working out at the gym or getting a massage, relax into the feeling that you and your ideal body are at one, sharing this moment. Feed your desire with your loving attention, and you will pull it close to you. Treat your desire like a dear friend coming to visit. Prepare a space for it. Think loving thoughts of it often. Greet and acknowledge it wherever you see it. And in the same way, love the idea of all of your future manifestations. Love the possibilities that will unfold in your life as they come into greater and greater view. Focus on why you want them, on the life-giving properties of how it feels to desire in the first place.

Within every desire are all the seeds that support its complete realization. The desire itself came loaded with everything needed to bring about its full realization. It is encoded like DNA. You don't need to add anything to it. You just need to tend it. Acknowledge it. Be mindful of its presence. Realize that because you desire it, it already exists within you. There is great sufficiency all around you. Flow your love toward everything in your life that is already working well, and appreciate what you already have enough of. This is how you open the doorway to greater abundance.

Chapter 5: The Principle of Loving— Applying It Step by Step

1   Begin by acknowledging that in this very moment, you already have a relationship with the object of your desire, and allow yourself to explore the quality of that relationship. When you think of your desire, are you more often

filled with feelings of eagerness and anticipation or feelings of frustration, hopelessness, or dread?

2 Allow yourself to notice what percentage of your daily thoughts, moods, and expectations contribute to a positive, good-feeling relationship with your desire. And notice also what percentage of your dominant thoughts are actually eroding or damaging it.

3 In this moment, what is "good enough" about this aspect of your life? What is working? What do you easily accept and appreciate? What are you thankful for?

4 Envision yourself living the full expression of your desire, and allow yourself to feel love and appreciation for all that you have drawn into your experience. Say to yourself, "Oh, how I love what I see! I love the joyous expressions and the happy scenes. I love doing what I love to do. I love being who I want to be. I love having what I want to have. I love the images of total fulfillment that I am now seeing in my mind and feeling in my heart." Give thanks for your clarity, your receptivity, and your ability to create.

5 Acknowledge that there is a powerful chemistry and connection that exists between you and this as-yet-unmanifested desire, and this energy is *alive*. Invite it to interact with you, to guide you, and to call you toward it. Use the following exercise to help you do this.

Energy Mastery Exercise

Dressing Yourself Up in Love

*B*egin by placing your body in a position of comfort. Adjust your arms, your shoulders, your back . . . position your legs and feet in a way that maximizes your experience of relaxation and comfort. Allow your spine to be straight and your jaw to loosen. Bring forth the intention to fall still, to drop into and feel your body for a moment, releasing any areas of tightness and finding comfort and peace in your physical experience.

Take a breath in, and imagine that you are relaxing at an even deeper level. Let that wave of relaxation travel down your face, down your jaw, into your neck and shoulders. Relax your arms and hands. Let a wave of relaxation spread to all the muscles in your back and stomach. Feel your breathing growing deeper and more relaxed.

Feel yourself letting go of the outside world and going deep within. Declare this as a sacred time for you to replenish, recharge, and reconnect. You are comfortable and serene. Your emotions are growing calmer and more tranquil. Your mind is becoming clear, reflecting the higher planes of reality like a clear mountain lake that is reflecting the clouds high above. Your mind is able to receive and transmit the clear light of your higher self. The Divine's thoughts are becoming one with your thoughts.

And with your next deep breath, call into your mind's eye an image of your desire having already been brought into full manifestation and fruition. See yourself doing, being, having, and enjoying the object of your desire. Feel the feelings that are associated with its fulfillment. Do you feel happy? Lighthearted? Excited? Joyful?

Breathe into these beautiful feelings, knowing that they are divine gifts for you to create and manifest and enjoy.

And now, allow these feelings to expand. Add color, sound, sensation, and dimension to the beautiful image you are conjuring in your mind. Allow your senses to drink it all in. Imprint every detail associated with the fulfillment of this desire, knowing that what you are seeing is even now making its way from energy into form, from the invisible world that sources all things into the full three-dimensional manifestation you desire. Imagine lifting up your vision to an even higher frequency, and imagine the highest, lightest, and most fulfilling scenes that your mind can conceive. Feel the excitement of seeing your desire already fulfilled. See it. Feel it. Know it.

And now, as you are basking in these beautiful images and sensations, allow yourself to actually fall in love with what you see. Feel your heart expand, the way it does when you think about someone you love, or see an image of something you cherish and adore. Allow that warm and beautiful feeling of love to move from your heart and radiate through the images in your mind. Feel the pure vibration of your love bringing these images to life, nurturing them like water and sunlight nourish a thriving plant. Love what you see with deep feeling.

And with another breath, acknowledge that through this vibration of love, which is the most powerful force in the universe, you are actually uniting the consciousness of the Divine with your personality consciousness. You are a powerful cocreator of your desire, the important human counterpart of the Divine's desire to live through you and as you. Feel this union.

And now, either silently or out loud, affirm to yourself, "I love what I see. I love the joyful expressions and happy scenes of my desire embodied in my present life experience. I love doing what I love to do. I love being what I want to be. I love having what I want to have. I love the pictures of total fulfillment that I am now seeing in my mind and feeling in my heart." Remind yourself that having and being are two sides of the same coin. By shifting your being to the powerful frequency of love, you are calling all that you desire to have into your experience.

Remember that the object of your desire is not something you have to work to acquire. It is an energy frequency that you have the ability to allow yourself to tune in to, in this and in every moment. All of life is energy: Love is energy. Money is energy. Happiness is energy.

Take another long moment to bask in this beautiful, life-giving energy of love, allowing it to penetrate every dimension of your body, your mind, your emotions, and your spirit. Feel yourself growing more magnetic to all that you wish to experience. Affirm to yourself that joyful abundance in all forms is your divine birthright. Take as much time as feels good to linger in your inner world, and when you are ready, slowly begin to open your eyes and come back to your present time and place. As you move into the next segment of your day, feel yourself bringing with you the all-attractive energy of love.

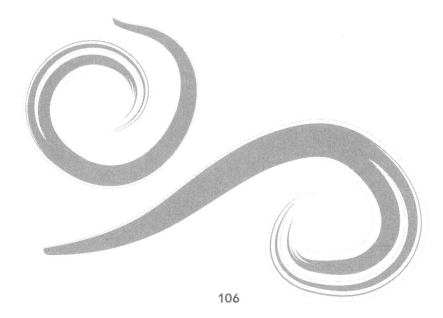

6

The Principle of Surrender

*Surrender is necessary to be an energy master and to
deliberately create the life you desire. You will have contrast that
shows up in your experience of life, and it is all a gift for you. It is
not that you are being punished, or that something is wrong with
you. It is an opportunity to return back into alignment with your
Divine Self . . . always. And surrendering what is in the way of that
connection is essential for your growth, and expansion, and your
desires being fulfilled. Open up the gift. Receive the information
it holds for you. And have faith that the universe loves and adores
you and wants your greater good, because it does.*

The Quantum Council

*I*n an ideal world, we would all remain in a state of genuinely
loving and appreciating our desires—those that have manifested into full tangible form as well as those that are still making
their way into our three-dimensional experience. Because, as we

explored in the previous chapter, the act of loving makes us irresistibly attractive and effortlessly magnetizes to us all the necessary components needed to fulfill our desires.

But what about those situations in which we've clearly fallen out of the vibration of love? What if we've wanted a particular desire to manifest for so long or with such intensity that its absence is actually painful to us? What can we do when we're standing smack dab in the middle of a manifestation that is not a reflection of our desire but a blatant reflection of its exact opposite? How do we keep impatience and self-doubt from creeping in when it feels like it's taking forever for a particular desire to come about?

The understanding that in every moment and with every vibration we offer, we are either aligning with or blocking our desires from coming into easy fruition begs an important question that this chapter promises to answer: When things are not going as we would like, and we realize that we are the ones getting in our own way, what is the best course of action we can take? The Principle of Surrender provides these very answers, as it holds the next essential piece of wisdom along your journey of deliberate creation and energy mastery.

When contrasting experiences arise and we feel the tension, disappointment, frustration, or fear that lets us know that our outer reality is currently out of alignment with an inner desire we hold dear, we can respond to this discord in one of two ways. We can become fixated on everything that appears to be going wrong or on the perspective that we can't have or attain our desire, or we can use the clarity of this contrasting experience to sharpen our focus and recalibrate our point of attraction. The latter choice brings us relief and soothing that opens the doorway to more pleasing manifestations. The former choice holds us in an even stronger state of resistance.

When things feel like they're going sideways—whether in our careers, in our finances, in our intimate relationships, or in relation to some personal improvement we're working to bring about within ourselves—the natural tendency is to take a detailed accounting of everything that is unwanted and to then set out on a path to change the people or circumstances we believe to be the cause of our discontent. After all, if other people or the universe at large would just give us what we want, we'd feel better, right?! This belief that we need circumstances to change in order to relieve our discontent gives rise to thoughts like *If only I could finally meet the man or woman of my dreams . . .* or *If only my current partner were more attentive . . .* or *If only the people at work would respect me, or if my family could just understand how many obstacles I've overcome . . .* all compelling arguments for sure. And every one of them serves only to increase our experience of powerlessness and limitation.

Another common option, when we find ourselves without something we want or in the presence of something we don't, is to decide that we are the ones who have acted inappropriately and that's why we're not getting what we want. We might believe that there is something wrong with us, or that the universe is not on our side, and we are therefore undeserving of having our desires manifest. We may beat ourselves up for losing sight of our goal, or for not trying hard enough. We might even wander down the rabbit hole of feeling incapable or unworthy as we recall the painful memories of similar past mistakes.

A third and equally disempowering response when our desires haven't yet manifested is to resign ourselves to the idea that what we want is out of our reach, that it simply wasn't meant to be. In this case, we attempt to do the impossible, which is to stifle the desire that's been born within us. This often seems the most rational way out of our discomfort, especially if our perception is that we were happier before we acknowledged having the desire. And so, in an attempt to feel better, we try to pull our desire back, only to discover that once life has helped us identify something we want, we can never disconnect ourselves from that expanded awareness.

But to take any of these courses of action—however justified or warranted they may seem—only widens the gap between the reality we're currently living and the reality we deeply desire to create.

The Gap between Desire and Belief

There is a gap between where you want to be and where you currently stand. There is a gap between what your heart knows is possible and the results you've managed to produce to date. There is a gap between the person you want more than anything to become and the person you show up as on a day-to-day basis.

This gap exists on multiple levels simultaneously. Yes, it exists in the realm of space and time. For example, you may want a million

dollars in the bank right now, but
there will likely be a gap of time
before you can realize this desire
completely. And the gap exists also
in the realm of belief: you may want
to wear a size 6 in clothing but believe
it's impossible because of family genetics,
a metabolic imbalance, or even your own
personal history. What's vital to understand is
that the gap between what you desire and what you
currently have does not exist "out there." It exists in consciousness.

Your experience of the gap is created by your perception. Are
you focusing on the result or on all the obstacles that you perceive
are blocking you from getting there? Your answer to this will determine the ease of your manifestations. Focusing on the result and the
vibration of having it creates an open line for the universe to manifest it. But when our beliefs, our doubts, and our past experiences
are focused on the gap, it seems to prove that what we want will
never come to be. And our experience of it is made more real—and
increasingly more uncomfortable—every time we focus on the pain
of not yet having what we want.

Big Asking Widens the Gap

Whenever you ask for something that is far beyond what you currently have—like a dramatic increase in prosperity or an ideal,
healthy relationship when you've just come out of a string of horrible relationships—the gap between where you now are and what
you really want becomes even more pronounced. But the real distance that we're seeking to bridge is *not* the distance between debt

and prosperity or between an unhealthy relationship and a healthy one. Bridging the gap between where we are and where we want to be is only a matter of soothing the discord in our own vibration.

Before you can be receptive to the new and improved outcome you've been asking for, you must get vibrationally up to speed with your own desire. So, to return to our previous example of manifesting a healthy, ideal relationship when all of your past relationships have been undesirable or unhealthy, accomplishing this is going to require a shift in your personal vibration. You will have to go through the process of becoming a person who is a vibrational match to the person you want to attract.

If you're currently living paycheck to paycheck but what you really want is to become financially independent, you will first have to locate and become practiced at the vibration of abundance before the abundance you seek can come to you. And if you've never been in an amazing intimate relationship but desire to be, you'll have to invest some creative energy into imagining how that would look and feel. This is how you train your vibration into consistent harmony with what you want rather than with what you've got.

When the vibration of abundance—or love, or success, or whatever it is that your heart desires—becomes your automatic, natural, go-to vibrational set point, circumstances will begin to orchestrate themselves around it. By contrast, if you have not achieved a vibration that supports the reality you desire, that desire cannot become

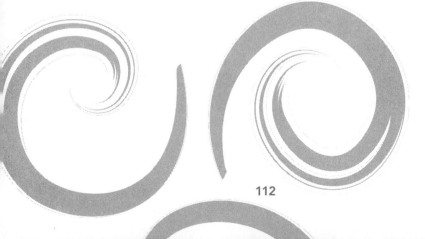

a lasting part of your life experience. In fact, anytime we attempt to change circumstances without first making the corresponding shift in our vibration, the changes either don't come about or are short-lived.

Do a simple Google search, and you'll find countless stories about lottery winners plucked out of the pits of financial hardship and dropped into a sudden windfall of cash. But within a couple of years or even months, they've either spent it all or lost it all and are back in the same situation they were in before winning the lottery. The same holds true for people who use willpower and action alone to effect a change in their fitness level or weight. They might spend hundreds or thousands of dollars on some program or special diet that promises results—and do manage to lose the weight. But the moment they go back to eating in a normal fashion, the weight returns. In both cases, the desired results were not sustainable because the vibrational work was not accomplished prior to taking the action.

You have to bring yourself internally up to speed with the vibration of your desire before that desire can manifest and remain a part of your outer reality. Nothing new can come into your life unless you open yourself up to it on an energetic level. And by the same token, anything in the world that you're open to on an energetic level can be yours, regardless of your age, your past, your education, or your circumstances. Regardless even of who you know or how much effort you put in. Remember, it's the vibration you are sending out that the universe is responding to. Vibration is primary; manifestations follow.

Everyone can relate to the experience of the gap between desire and belief, and for some of us, our early childhood experiences were filled with this sense of longing. To some extent, the gap is an inherent part of the process of creation, because every time we set a new goal or acknowledge a new desire, we naturally become more aware of all the places where our current reality falls short. But remember that because the limitless source is always matching the vibrations that we send out, our desires are in the process of manifesting—perhaps in a way even better than we imagined.

When the Gap Is Leading You to Something Bigger

Sometimes when we're experiencing the gap between where we are and what we want, it's not a sign of misalignment. Sometimes it just means that there is a bigger plan for us, a more perfect timeline that the universe is working to unfold on our behalf. When we've been trying hard to manifest something and it still isn't happening, it often means there's an easier way to accomplish what we desire than the handful of possibilities that our minds have considered. Just know that whenever you're pushing hard and not getting the results you desire, it's time to surrender. In that state of surrender, you become receptive and the intelligence of the universe can more easily guide you. I have had many profound experiences of this in my own life.

Before I met my husband, Frederic, I was in an eight-year relationship with my first husband, and the whole time we were together, I wanted more than anything to become a mom. In fact, I had desired this all my life. We began trying soon after we got married, and because I was so young, I assumed I would get pregnant right away. When after several months it still hadn't happened, I began applying the spiritual knowledge I had at that time to facilitate the fulfillment of this desire.

I scripted the exact life I envisioned myself living, picturing myself as a mom who has the freedom to nurture and play with my baby while also attending to my at-home coaching practice, developing programs, and expanding my career. I saw myself trotting out to the mailbox with my baby in my arms and collecting checks that were delivered in the mail. I envisioned the fulfillment of this desire in every detail, and I felt it as if it were already a reality.

In the year that followed, there were many times when I intuitively felt I was pregnant, but it never came to fruition. Other times, I was sure I had had a miscarriage, but even that could not be confirmed. I was growing more discouraged by the day. I was doing everything I knew to do, and still this very soul-level desire was not coming to fruition. I could not envision myself going down the path of in vitro fertilization or other fertility treatments. Of course, there is nothing whatsoever wrong with those paths, and I've known and coached many women for whom it was the perfect avenue. It was just not something that I felt called to do for myself.

During this time, I felt like I was walking through glue. Every step I took and every effort I made toward the realization of my desire seemed to be taking me backward. Finally, after more than a year of trying and failing, my then-husband made a confession: he didn't actually want kids! He had a child from a previous marriage who was twelve years old at the time, and he wasn't eager to go through the "baby stage" again. No wonder I felt as though I was walking through glue! When he got a vasectomy, it felt like the death of a dream—but my desire was still very much alive.

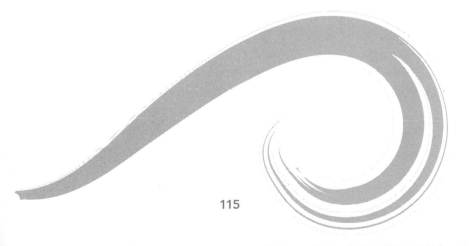

After this devastating blow, I did what I coach all my clients to do. I turned my attention to other aspects of my life that felt creative and expansive, into which I could pour my love and my heart. I became an even more devoted student of universal laws. I continued to build my coaching practice. I wrote my first book, which came to me, already written, in a series of downloads which I would later understand to be channeled information. My spiritual evolution continued at a rapid pace, and although I was still not a mother, I was growing more and more into the woman I had always wanted to be.

Soon another contrasting experience made itself known—my connection with my husband was beginning to unravel. You see, while I had been busy learning, growing, and expanding both personally and professionally, he had stayed pretty much the same. Our relationship no longer felt right, and it was clear that we were not growing together as a couple. I was headed in a direction that was right for me, but the person I was with was going somewhere else. We were no longer a vibrational match.

With this growing realization, I began to focus with even greater intent on connecting with and aligning with my inner being. I surrendered my attachment to what I thought my life was supposed to look like and consciously gave myself and my well-being over to the benevolence of the universe, trusting that even if the outer form of my life changed, my inner connection would guide me to a new expression that would better support the powerful, spiritual woman I was becoming.

One day, seemingly out of the blue (although I now know that nothing is!), my husband and I got into an argument. We had been talking about what each of us wanted out of our relationship, and something I said offended him—to the extent that he refused to talk to me for the next three days. I used the solitude to immerse myself deeper into my spiritual practices . . . meditating, journaling, and purifying my vibration through practicing forgiveness and self-love. On the third day of his silent treatment, I went to him and said, "This isn't working," meaning that I no longer wanted to experience the stress of living under the same roof and avoiding one another. Immediately, he took off his wedding ring, threw it at me, and said, "Fine. I'll give you a divorce!" At first I was stunned; divorce had never even crossed my mind. But a moment later, a sense of peace began to wash over me. I could feel the freedom and the rightness of it. I swiftly filed the paperwork.

As the months passed, living in the small town of Redding, California, where my ex had been born and raised, no longer felt like a fit for me either. I was constantly running into his friends and family members around town, including even one who was a member at my gym and was extremely cold and rude to me. I had no idea where I wanted to live; I just knew I wanted to be far away from where I was. The smallness and familiarity of it felt stifling to me. I began praying to the universe for some sort of sign.

One day, after bumping into my ex's friend at my gym yet again and feeling judged and ridiculed, the gap between where I was and where I wanted to be widened even further, and my desire to move reached a new intensity. Intuitively, I knew my discomfort was productive. It was leading me to something—I just didn't yet know what. It's like I could sense a parallel reality in which the possibilities I was reaching for were right there for the taking but were still hidden behind a veil, just out of sight. Sitting in my car before I finished my last sales call for the day, I surrendered into the unknown and prayed to become receptive enough to pick up on whatever was next for me.

When I returned home from work that evening, there was an email waiting for me from the pharmaceutical company where I worked as a sales rep, announcing that they were looking for a sales training manager to work out of their Philadelphia office. Now, if you were to look at a map of the United States and draw a horizontal line heading east from Redding, California, you'd make the same discovery I made that day. Philadelphia, Pennsylvania, is just about as far as one can get from Redding, California, without crossing an ocean! I booked the flight, interviewed for the position, and got the job—along with a nice bump in pay. Plus, I was now living on the East Coast, which meant I had easy access to an entirely new lineup of coaching and leadership programs—very much in alignment with my Desire Factor at the time. Four months later, at one such leadership program, I met my amazing husband, Frederic. And of course, starting a family was one of his deep heartfelt desires too.

Within months of trying to get pregnant, we did—and it was just as easy when it was time for our second child too. That was over ten years ago, and now our family of four is living out almost the exact script I created all those years ago, while in the midst of an unfulfilling marriage. I am a mom who has the flexibility to spend quality time with my family, as well as the opportunity to run an international coaching business and conduct presentations and seminars all over the world. I love what I do, I love where I live, and I have plenty of time to write, to create, to coach, and to produce my internet TV show—all from the comfort of my home, and all with my children and gorgeous husband in the next room! Everything I desired came to fruition because I had enough trust in the universe to surrender my "perfect pictures" of how I thought my life should look, surrendering also my ideas about the perfect timeline.

When obstacles to our desires appear in our path, like those I encountered with my first husband, the Principle of Surrender has us take a step back and really ask ourselves, "What are the benefits of this obstacle? What can I learn from this? If this situation were actually unfolding in the perfect way and the perfect time, and for my highest good, what would that reason be?" I can promise you, there is always a reason. The Quantum Council, a collective consciousness of nonphysical ascended masters who I now serve as a messenger for, explains that the blocks that come up along the path to fulfilling our desires are actually like little gifts wrapped up from the universe, and it is up to us to unwrap them and discover the wisdom inside. It's our job to look within to discover why we are creating this obstacle, in what ways it's serving us, and what we can learn from it. This is exactly what I do in my own life. Anytime I find myself coming up against a wall, or feel like I'm moving through glue, I take a step back and go within.

Sometimes our Divine Self manifests obstacles in our path because it's trying to protect us in some way. As was the case with my ex-husband, sometimes our Desire Factor is right on, but the timing isn't right, or the person isn't right. When we hit up against those walls, the wise action is to surrender—not to try to force our way through the wall. Obstacles are placed on our path because there is something important we need to learn from them, some skill set or insight that we're being called to hone, because we're going to need it once our desire has manifested. And the obstacles to our desires are perfect catalysts to lead us to that very wisdom.

In an article called "Learn the Value of Spiritual Surrender," first published in *Yoga Journal* in 2007, author Sally Kempton suggests that these obstacles are a type of spiritual impasse that is leading us to something greater. She describes it in this way:

> You are trying as best you can to make something happen, and you're failing. You realize that you simply cannot do whatever it is you want to do, cannot win the battle you're in, cannot complete the task, cannot change the dynamics of the situation. At the same time, you recognize that the task must be completed, the situation must change. In that moment of impasse, something gives in you, and you enter either a state of despair or a state of trust. Or sometimes both: one of the great roads to the recognition of grace leads through the heart of despair itself.

To acknowledge the existence of the solution, even when you're knee-deep in the problem . . . to recognize that you're being called to greater expansion when you're living what feels like a devastating loss . . . to know that, because your desires are an expression of your Divine Self, you must continue to put your faith in them, even when there is no evidence that they're on track. This is the work of surrender.

Surrender and faith go hand in hand. They call us to believe in the viability of our desires and to keep moving toward them, even when the outer world seems to reflect something different. When we surrender to the path of our desire, even when we have no idea where it will lead, we emerge on the other side as much greater, more empowered versions of ourselves. And sometimes, that journey changes everything about us and redirects the entire trajectory of our lives. Another beautiful case in point:

Media icon Oprah Winfrey first learned about Alice Walker's award-winning novel, *The Color Purple*, one Sunday morning after

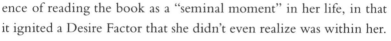

seeing a review about it in the *New York Times*. Still in her pajamas, Oprah put on a long coat and drove to the bookstore to buy it. She read the book in one day, then went back to the bookstore and bought every copy they had in stock. She gave one to everyone she knew and even carried around a backpack full of them to hand out to strangers. Oprah recalls the experience of reading the book as a "seminal moment" in her life, in that it ignited a Desire Factor that she didn't even realize was within her.

After the huge success of the book, Oprah began hearing rumors that plans for a movie were underway. Her reaction to this news surprised her. Despite the fact that she had never before acted in a feature film, she had a burning desire to land a role in the movie. She surrendered to this desire and allowed it to grow within her— even though it seemed unlikely—and began praying for a role in the film.

At this time, Oprah had just moved from Baltimore to Chicago to become the host of the morning news show *A.M. Chicago*. Unbeknownst to her, producer Quincy Jones, who was involved in casting the film, was in Chicago defending a lawsuit filed against Michael Jackson's *Thriller* album. As he was getting dressed in his hotel room, Jones turned on the TV, which just happened to be tuned to *A.M. Chicago*, and, taking one look at Oprah, said to himself right out loud, "*That's* Sofia." Jones immediately called his casting agent, who reached out to Oprah and offered an audition in a film he referred to as *Moon Song*. Keep in mind this was the early 1980s and Oprah had never received a call like this before in her life. Oprah responded, asking, "Are you sure you don't want me to audition for *The Color Purple*?" After all, *that* was the movie role she'd been thinking about, praying about, and even dreaming about for months. The casting agent reiterated the name of the film and gave Oprah the details.

When Oprah arrived at the audition and was given the script, she instantly recognized the storyline from *The Color Purple*. She had read the book cover to cover so many times and had such a passionate connection with the characters that she knew every detail of the story by heart. It turns out, *Moon Song* was a fictitious title—a common strategy used for keeping hush-hush film productions under wraps. What she was actually reading for was the role of Sofia in *The Color Purple*. Oprah completed the audition, but after two months went by and she hadn't heard anything, she began to lose hope.

Concluding that she didn't get the role because she was "fat" (she weighed about 212 pounds at that time), she checked herself into a weight-loss spa, determined to drop fifteen pounds quickly. She continued praying, this time asking God to help her release her desire to be in the movie because she'd become obsessed with it. "Please, help me let it go," she prayed.

One day, as she was running around the warm-up track, crying to be released from both her extra weight and her desire for the film role she believed she would not get, Oprah began singing the gospel song "I Surrender All" out loud as she ran. Her new goal was to release her attachment to this outcome she had wanted so badly to create, so she could get on with her life. Eventually, as she ran and sang and cried, she was able to envision the role of Sofia being played by another actress and not feel physically sick. A wave of resolution came over her, and she knew she would be able to go to the movie and enjoy it for the incredible story of courage and spiritual conviction it portrayed.

The instant she surrendered and knew everything would be all right—with or without her involvement in the movie—a woman came running outside to find her. "There's a phone call for you," the woman said, breathless. "The guy on the phone says he's Steven Spielberg."

"I hear you're at a fat farm," Spielberg said as Oprah picked up the phone. Then he continued, "I saw your audition for Sofia, and I would like to see you in my office tomorrow—and by the way, if you lose a single pound, you could lose this part." Now, for those who have seen the film, you know that Sofia's impressive stature is an integral part of what makes her character so fearless and powerful. Oprah packed her bags and checked out of that weight-loss camp in seven minutes flat, stopping at the Dairy Queen on her way to the audition. And the rest, as they say, is history. Oprah had this to say about the experience:

> *The Color Purple* changed my life. It changed everything about my life because, in that moment of praying and letting go, I really understood the principle of surrender. The principle of surrender is that, after you have done all that you can do, and you've done your best and given it your all, you then have to release it to whatever you call God, or don't call God. It doesn't matter what you call it because God doesn't care about a name. You just release it to that which is greater than yourself, and whatever is supposed to happen, happens. And I have used that principle about a million times now. You release it to Grace.

The Desire Is about Who You Become

The gap between what we desire and what we're currently living will continue to exist, because we are continually evolving. But it's who we become as we navigate this gap that brings the true joy in life—or the despair.

Do we allow the gap to rob us of our passion, using it as justification to abandon our desires? Do we give in to the opinions of others, who insist that what we want isn't possible, that we're too fat, too old, too young, too uneducated or inexperienced? Or do we boldly, courageously allow our desires to live on within us, with faith that they will lead us where we ultimately want to go?

Remember where your heartfelt desire came from in the first place. They are sparks that come forth from your Divine Self, ignited within you for the purpose of expanding you into all that you are capable of being. I think of each person's specialized desires as spiritual bread crumbs provided by source to lead each of us upon our unique paths of expansion. The moment we recognize that spiritual bread crumb on our path, our personalities light up and send a resounding message through our entire being that says, "Yes! I want that!" Intuitively we know that the pursuit of it will bring us greater joy, freedom, or exhilaration of life. That is the true purpose of desire. Oprah was a morning talk show host with no prior acting experience when the desire to star in a major motion picture stranded on her heart. She surrendered to it, and the journey it took her on changed her life forever. The same holds true for each individual desire that is born within any one of us.

My hair and makeup stylist has a burning desire to run a marathon, and I have no doubt that who she will become in the process of surrendering to this desire will lead her to greater joy and self-empowerment . . . and I know this even though nowhere in my being do I hold that same desire! All of our desires are unique. All are worth believing in and surrendering to, whether it's the desire to run a marathon, to trek across Europe with only a backpack, to learn a second language, or to win a million dollars as a contestant on a game show.

There is no need to judge any of our desires as being important or unimportant, superficial or meaningful, or spiritual or materialistic. They are all bread crumbs left for us by our Divine Selves to lead us to greater joy and satisfaction. It's all about this continual process of becoming, and—as far as I can tell—it never ends.

The universe holds a bird's-eye view of our lives and is more than capable of managing all the pieces of the puzzle that make up what each of us considers to be our ideal and perfect whole. When we surrender our need to figure out how, who, what, when, and where it will happen, and we place our attention instead on simply aligning ourselves in heart and mind to the essence of our desire, the universe makes it happen for us. There is no pushing, shoving, manipulating, planning, or any of the other strategies that we've been taught to use to go after what we want.

And so, if your desire is to create larger streams of money and abundance, or to increase your stamina and become healthier, you have to wear the energy of what it feels like to be living in that reality, the same way you would wear a piece of clothing. Think of it as taking off the frumpy energy suit you've been wearing (you know, the one that smacks of *not good enough, tries too hard,* or *unworthy*) and

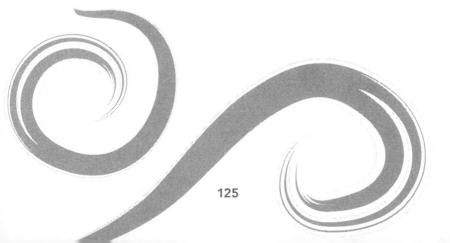

literally stepping into a brand-new suit that is perfectly suited to the reality you are in the process of creating. You're stepping into a new realm of possibility, a new bandwidth of frequency. And as a result, you now have access to a whole new energy field where the components of what you desire can be realized by you.

You first have to connect with the feeling essence of what you desire, and then you have to own that feeling by wearing it, being it, and taking it with you everywhere you go. In other words, you must reach beyond the realm of what already is and anchor yourself in the realm where everything you desire already exists.

It's easy to feel loved when you're in a great relationship, but when you've been single for years, achieving this feeling state requires more focus. In the same way, it's easy to feel abundant when money is rolling in, but what about when you're in a bad financial situation or worried about your job security or the strength of the economy? These are the moments when we have to look beyond the conditions that have already manifested and find the unconditional essence of our desires. Honing this skill is what makes us deliberate creators. We become visionaries who chart our own courses instead of travelers who simply follow the paths that have already been charted.

You didn't come here to simply observe reality or to limit your desires to what's been created before. You didn't come here to find yourself at the mercy of the status quo or to ask other people to change their ways so that you can get the things you want. And you didn't take a body to allow other people's opinions to determine the height of your ceiling. You came here to be the creator of your own reality, to live in this three-dimensional world with full knowledge that the higher dimensions of life are the source of everything that happens on this one. You are that larger being, that Divine Self. You came here to apply your spiritual understanding and creative prowess to impact and transform physical reality, not to permit physical reality to diminish the potency of your creations.

You are ready to claim your full understanding and mastery of the spiritual dimension from which all things come. You're ready to surrender the illusion that only things that can be seen, heard, tasted, and touched are "real" and to acknowledge the earliest beginnings of your full-blown manifestations before they are tangible enough for anyone to see. You're ready to believe in what you desire while it's still in its invisible vibrational state, to surrender your allegiance to the constantly changing world of form and to place your faith in that which is still unseen.

Contrast—or the experience of being in the gap—is a powerful invitation to continue practicing the vibration of what we desire while simultaneously releasing our attachment to how it will unfold. By actively surrendering into the expansion that the contrast is pointing us toward, we shorten the duration between the birth of a desire and its fulfillment—and we discover the key to soothing our own discomfort along the way.

Chapter 6: The Principle of Surrender—
Applying It Step by Step

1   As you contemplate the area of your life that is the focus of your current Desire Factor, acknowledge the ways in which you are experiencing a gap between what you desire and the circumstances you are now living.

2   As you feel this point of tension between where you are and where you would like to be, acknowledge the clarity that has been born from it. What is it that you do want

to experience in this area of your life? Identify both the material changes you desire to make ("I want to get out of debt") as well as the immaterial ("I want to feel at ease and secure").

3 Acknowledge the ways that the obstacles or setbacks you have encountered have actually served as a catalyst for your growth. What awareness, clarity, or wisdom do you now possess as a direct result of having lived this contrast? What changes have you been inspired to make?

4 Remember that every situation is made up of two polarities—that which is wanted and that which is not wanted—and you are the one with the power to decide on which end of this spectrum you place your focus. Choose to use this contrast the way the universe intended—to conjure within you the feeling of your desire already being fulfilled. The following exercise will help you do this.

Energy Mastery Exercise

Purifying the Energy of Your Desire

Begin by taking a nice, deep breath in, and as you exhale, allow yourself to come more fully into this moment. Allow yourself to feel the relief of turning your attention inward, letting go of any thoughts about your day, letting go of any thoughts about the future, and just surrendering yourself to this moment and to this experience. Continue to rest your attention on the in and out of your breath, knowing that your breath is the bridge that connects your physical self with the nonphysical, infinite, energetic being that you are.

Call forth the intention to use this process to make yourself more of a vibrational match to the object of your desire and to release any contradicted energy within you that may be unconsciously holding you apart from it. Take another deep breath in, and let it all the way out. Allow yourself to notice the points of gravity that are holding your body in the chair that you are sitting in. Allow yourself to feel heavy, to feel supported. Notice how good it feels to make yourself the object of your own attention, and really thank yourself for taking this time to acknowledge and nourish the connection between you and you.

And now, with another deeper breath, softly bring forth an image or thought form about the object of your desire, and allow yourself to objectively notice how you're perceiving it. Just breathe in and become aware of where you now are in relation to that desire, how you feel about it, the thoughts that are moving through your mind about it. Just allow yourself to gather this information without censoring or judging it, knowing that increasing your awareness about what's happening is the first step to shifting your experience. So just become aware of any thoughts that come up and the feelings those thoughts produce within you. If you're feeling any disappointment or frustration, allow yourself to feel it, reminding yourself that it's just contradicted energy and that acknowledging this disconnection is necessary in order to extract the gifts from it. Give yourself permission to feel your own energy field and allow it to be exactly as it is in this moment.

And with another deep breath, see if you can grant your feelings even more permission to be. Just accept that they are there, that this is the mix of vibrations that is currently within you, and accept whatever emotions are present without judgment. Give yourself total permission to feel what you feel. Bring a beginner's mind and an open heart to whatever experience is unfolding for you. See if you can accept that every experience is a gift—even though it may not feel like it in the moment—and that your job is to be open to the gift and receive it. By accepting rather than resisting whatever emotions are present for you, you surrender your resistance and are able to then release the energy contained within the emotions.

Use your breath to bring all of your awareness and attention into your emotional body, feeling the sensations that are present in your belly, your chest, and your heart. It's not necessary to name the emotions, to justify them, to explain them, or even to tell a story about them. Just feel the pulsation of the energy that is moving through your emotional body. And let yourself pulsate with it. It's just energy, and you are making the powerful choice to surrender into this energy rather than to place yourself in opposition to it.

You may feel an increase in intensity or feel your body temperature change slightly. Keep using your breath to allow this process to unfold within you, and give it as much time as is required. Allow yourself to get to a place of full acceptance of and surrender to the emotion, and notice as you begin to feel a release of the pulsation. Again, use your breath to allow the sensation to change. Trust the process that is unfolding.

Take another slow, deep breath, and again call into your awareness the soft presence of your desire. Feel the energy of it. Notice that this reality vibrates at a particular frequency, and your desire is the vehicle that is calling you up to this higher frequency. Allow yourself to see and feel the pulsating vibration of your heart's desires. Feel yourself connecting with it on an energetic level. You are harmonizing and becoming one with the vibration of your desire.

And now allow yourself to become aware of any actions that would support you in integrating even further with the vibration of your desire. What thoughts, emotions, and attitude would align you even further? What communications could you initiate that would establish you more firmly in this higher frequency? If you were completely at one with the energy of your desire, what choices, practices, and actions would you naturally and easily take? Just allow yourself to receive any messages that want to come through, knowing that you may perceive these messages with one of your senses or with your sixth sense of intuition or with a quiet knowing.

And then, coming back once again to your breath, bring into your awareness the essence of your desire. Why do you desire this particular object, condition, or experience? What feeling state do you believe you will experience as a result? Is it self-respect, love, faith, connection? Allow your focus to recalibrate back on what you want and why you want it, letting the why bring you into a state of alignment with your desire.

Acknowledge that everything you desire to experience—whether it's satisfaction or fulfillment, joy, ease, happiness, creativity, compassion, freedom, love, or well-being—is available to you in this right-now, present moment. Allow yourself to become aware of anything you could do or focus on in the days ahead to continue to expand your consciousness to the frequency of your desire. Affirm to yourself these simple statements of truth:

- The universe has enough for everyone.

- There is more than enough to go around.

- My abundance does not diminish anyone else's experience.

- I deserve to create everything my heart desires.

Take another long moment to thank yourself for giving yourself the gift of your own attention and to acknowledge how powerful you are when you seek to master your own energy. Energy is the birthplace of everything, and you have just deliberately shifted yours into a state of greater allowing. Feel the power and the pride of that.

And when you are ready, gently begin to return your awareness to the room you are in, bringing back with you a deeper love and appreciation for who you are. Return your attention to your breath, breathing the light of your beautiful soul into you and out again into the world.

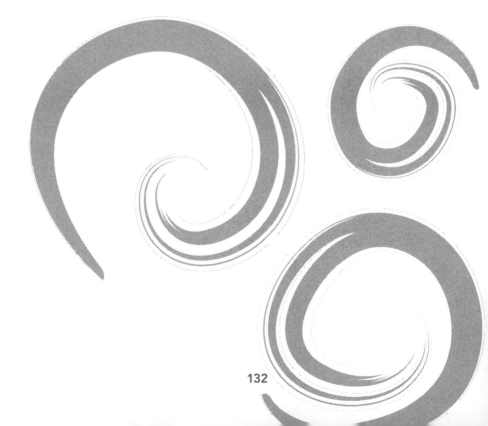

7

The Principle of Action

*You are cocreating with your Divine Self. Your Divine Self will
give you the idea and desire, will be the source of the energy
needed to flow to the desire, will guide you on what to do and
when, and will bring it into perfect timing and form. Your job is
to take the inspired action given to you. You are the eyes, ears,
arms, and hands of the Divine. You are the physical extension
of this partnership. Your inner and outer action is essential
for the attainment of all your desires.*

The Quantum Council

So here we are. The six principles that have come before have
been building blocks leading to the exact plateau where we
now stand, and we're ready to consider the final piece to the manifestation puzzle. By applying the principles of alignment, focus, joyful
expectancy, having, loving, and surrender, we place ourselves into
a receptive and pliable state in which we are open to the universal
intelligence that is, in every moment, guiding us to the fulfillment

of our desires. This guidance comes to us in the form of inspired thoughts, words, ideas, and emotions—all of which propel us powerfully forward into action.

In a state of internal alignment and receptivity, the energy summoned by our desires is allowed to flow freely, and as a result, it picks up speed all on its own. When we're aligned, we not only have access to the full range of our own resources, but we're also receptive to a higher stream of consciousness where all solutions and innovations are born. Actions that are taken after we've deliberately fostered a personal environment of alignment yield results that are so radically disproportionate to the effort expended, some may label them as miraculous. But what cannot be seen through physical eyes is the energetic alignment that was already in place long before the action was ever taken.

Action is the stage at which all that has previously been invisible to our physical senses can now be seen, heard, smelled, tasted, and touched. It's the point at which the creative energy we've already set into motion finally breaks through into manifested form, in the same way that a seed planted deep in the ground eventually sprouts up through the soil. Although we are just now seeing it, that seed has been maturing underground, quietly gathering strength and momentum for quite some time. And the same is true of all the invisible energy we flow in the direction of our desires.

The Principle of Action is a natural culmination and continuation of the six principles that come before. It is the tipping point at which the inner guidance we've received is ripe and ready to burst onto the scene in the outer world.

The moment a desire is born within us, the vibration of it creates a ripple effect that reverberates through all of the universe. Like when a rock is dropped into a still pond, the resulting waves will eventually make their way to the shore. And in the same way, once a desire has taken up residence in our consciousness, there really is no stopping its continued evolution. The movement of our desire toward its full realization occurs first at a vibrational level, and in the beginning stages of this movement, we may not even be aware of it. But once that vibration has gathered enough momentum that it begins generating thoughts, ideas, and impulses within us, it is up to us to do our part to keep that energy moving. For example, my desire to own that Coach purse all those years ago set off a series of actions—from quitting smoking to becoming more physically active to updating my wardrobe—all of which led me in the direction of becoming the woman I wanted to be. Action is the way the energy of our desire continues its forward motion along its trajectory from the unseen to the seen.

The Dance between Physical and Nonphysical

Action is the physical counterpart to the nonphysical source from which all abundance and creative energy flows. When we are open to the impulses being offered to us from the nonphysical source and respond to them through inspired physical action, we keep the energy circuit between our Divine Self and our human self open—and our desires manifest easily. And if we don't do our part to keep this circuit open, we interrupt the flow and the energy either withdraws or becomes stagnant and blocked.

Remember that you are an extension of the universe at large. If you're not willing to do your part, if you're not willing to act when you receive the calling, you are in effect short-circuiting the natural energy flow between the nonphysical and the physical. In other words, we have to meet the universe halfway. We send out a request, or offer an intention—*I desire X, Y, or Z*—which is transmitted energetically to the far corners of the energetic universe. But the other, equally important, side of this equation is that we have to be willing to allow what we have asked for or intended. We have to be willing to receive the inspiration and follow through with action—even when that action doesn't appear to lead in a straight line to what we desire.

The desire to write this book was born within me several years before I finally began writing it. I actually tried to resist the idea because I wasn't sure I was ready to make the commitment of energy and focus it takes to receive a message. But my Desire Factor persisted; the momentum continued building, and—not wanting to block the flow of inspiration that was moving through me—I did my part and began taking action.

First, I put the book's premise into proposal form and reached out to my literary agent at the time, Carrie, telling her that I already had a contact at a large publishing house who knew about the book and was waiting to receive the proposal. Without even reading it, Carrie looked up the bookstore sales records for my last two books, and because those numbers reflected only a tiny percentage of the number of copies actually sold, decided not to send the proposal to the editor who was waiting for it. She'd already concluded it wouldn't sell and that she couldn't get me a six-figure book advance. Strike one!

Next I reached out to Ellen, the literary agent who had repped one of my earlier books and who had expressed a lot of interest in my last two titles. Ellen read the proposal and loved the idea but passed because she was also going off reported book sales and not actual, so she didn't think she could get me a six-figure advance either. I explained to her that I wasn't interested in a six-figure advance and that I just wanted to find a publishing home for this book and the one that will follow, but she was looking only at the immediate monetary gain, not the long-term picture. Strike two.

A couple of days went by, and I was in meditation, in communion with the collection of nonphysical expanded consciousness that call themselves the Quantum Council. Toward the end of that meditation, I received an idea in the form of an image that flashed across the screen of my mind. I saw myself sending an email to Arielle Ford, who had been a successful literary agent for many years but was by then busy writing her own books and doing other things. The Council suggested that I email Arielle to ask her to rep this book. So I did. Arielle's email reply came back in less than a minute. "No way, no how!" was her poetic response. The days of repping authors and pitching books were long behind her, she explained. Strike three.

What the hell?! I thought. Here I was with a clear desire, not a frivolous one but a desire with a good deal of momentum and energy behind it, one which was inspiring what felt like logical and clear actions from me. Obediently I had followed through on each of these impulses, and each had turned out—or so it seemed—to be a dead end. Had I misinterpreted the impulses I was receiving? Had I moved into action before giving the energy enough time to build? I asked the Council about this, and they replied, clearly and calmly, that nothing had gone wrong. Each of these actions was a part of the process of manifestation, and each of them had played a part in getting the energy moving. By taking these actions, they explained, I had opened up a portal that allowed the energy of my desire to flow in a more concentrated way.

A couple of days later, I was having a conversation with a colleague and friend, Kelly, and told her about my experience of not being able to find a home for my new book and how frustrated I felt. "Christy," she said, "your books have hit the *New York Times* bestseller list not once but twice. There is no way you're having trouble finding a publisher for your latest book!" Kelly then asked if I wanted to be introduced to her literary agent, Devra—uh, *yes!*— and said she would call her the minute we hung up the phone. She did, and it turned out that Devra not only knew who I was but was also friends with me on Facebook and had commented on a post I had shared about my dog the day before. I had never heard of this woman or known we were friends on Facebook until she also posted a photo of her dog in response to my photo. We got on a call the same day and had a great connection; Devra got this book immediately, and within two weeks, she had found this book the publishing home I'd been looking for.

And what was even more interesting and magical to discover is the fact that it was Arielle Ford who first encouraged Devra years ago to become a literary agent! What?! In hindsight I could see that the impulse to connect with Arielle was actually a critical piece of the unfolding of this desire— as were the conversations I'd had with my previous agents and my colleague—even though these actions led me in very different directions than I initially thought or hoped they would.

Action gives us the opportunity to serve as the arms and legs of the Divine. It is the part we are assigned in the cocreative process and one that we cannot overlook if we want to bring our desires to their full manifestation. From my human and limited vantage point of what is and isn't possible, I could see only a handful of ways to fulfill my desire to find a publisher for this book. My mind was limited by what it believed it already knew. But because the Divine—which is pure, unbounded potentiality—gave me the desire, it also gave me the impulses, the ideas, and the inspiration to act in order to bring it to fruition in a way that was beyond anything I knew was possible.

Where the Rubber Hits the Road

Some who study and practice the Law of Attraction misinterpret one of its main precepts. Regardless of what some teachers of it advocate, it is not enough to simply sit around, visualizing and believing. We have to demonstrate trust in our desires by first receiving the inner guidance and next by taking action on them. Consider this: If you're dead set about manifesting something you desire without offering any action on your part—as many Law of Attraction students actually are—just think of the energetic stance you are placing yourself in. You're defying the universe to give you something you want while you yourself are not a cooperative participant in its unfolding. Remember, you are equal parts nonphysical and physical. And action is the physical link that brings the vibration of your desire into the three-dimensional world of form. And every time you follow through on an impulse and see the results—as I did with the publishing of this book—you increase your ability to trust and believe in yourself and the very deliberate role you are here to play in the process of manifestation.

There comes a point in every act of creation when it's time to pick up the pen, to make the call, to download the app, or to follow through on that hunch. The physical component of manifestation is every bit as important as the nonphysical. Taking action is the way the energy continues to move, to pick up speed, and to become. If you don't accept the gift of the desire, the energy of it will lose momentum and eventually return back to its source. The way you accept it is by allowing the energy to inspire you to action. This is the point at which, as they say, the rubber hits the road.

Action is the tipping point, where the energetic momentum has gathered so much velocity that it simply must evolve into something physical. It's the point at which there is so much focused intention, excitement, and positive expectation around the desire that to stay still would be unnatural. You are leaning so much into your desire and have so much energy invested in it that at a certain point, you can no longer stay cooped up at the starting gate. You are imbued with clarity and are so single-mindedly focused on the result you're committed to creating that it would take really a lot of opposing energy to knock you off your game.

There's an old saying that you've probably heard: if you want to get something done, give it to someone who's busy. This expression really speaks to the momentum of action. What it means is that when someone already has an established pattern of vibration that they back up through action, they are more likely to keep that momentum in motion and less likely to drop the ball when you give them a task. They have already established themselves as the kind of person who gets things done. This is the signal they are sending out, and the universe responds to it. The same is true with action. When we're pushing against the stream, even one more task or to-do item added to the list can throw us into a tailspin, but when we're going with the current, when we're in the zone and firing on all cylinders, so to speak, there is truly no limit to what we can accomplish, because the energy of our desire is unopposed by resistance.

Actions that we take from this free-flowing state of being are not forced or motivated; they are inspired. Inspired actions just feel right—to the extent that once the impulse occurs, often the idea won't let loose of us until we follow it through. The energy is so strong that you simply can-not *not* take action. Inspired actions come as a flash of insight, a sudden urge, or intuition. Sometimes they occur as an emotional reaction that feels dispropor-tionate to whatever it is we're considering. We receive them as a "hell yes!"—as an impulse so strong that it bypasses the limitations of our rational, suspicious, or pessimistic minds. Going with the flow of inspired action is leveraging universal energy; that's why it feels more like play than work. We easily and joyfully get more done in less time. And our experience is exactly the opposite when our actions are motivated or forced.

Trying Too Hard

Motivated or forced actions are, unfortunately, a huge waste of time and energy. I say *unfortunately* because this truly is one of those cos-mic jokes—a vicious cycle that only an awareness of energy and universal law allows us to break out of. Anytime we feel the need to force ourselves into action, it's almost always because our perception is one of scarcity or lack. An important deadline is looming, per-haps, or maybe some event has triggered our instinctive survival urge and we feel as though we are up against a wall. Believing that we have few options—or feeling maybe that the universe has turned its back on us and it's up to us alone to make things happen—we throw our alignment out the window, roll up our proverbial sleeves, and force ourselves to act.

Excessive thinking is the watermark of forced action. We're out of alignment so the next step is not clear, but we feel compelled to act anyway. And so we act without clarity, without any aligned energy behind our actions. In that state, everything is hit-and-miss, like throwing mud at a wall and hoping some of it will stick, or like Chicken Little running around in circles, using a lot of energy but not going anywhere. Because we're in a perceived state of lack—or we're fearful that we will be soon—we feel pressured to do some-thing *now* to alleviate our stress.

My client Nick came to one of our recent coaching calls in this state. I felt the difference in him as soon as he started speaking. His

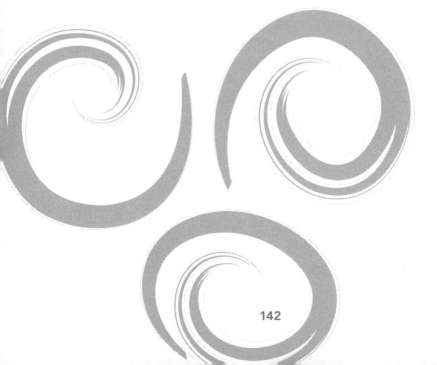

usual thoughtfulness and big-picture thinking were replaced with anxiety and a laser focus that constricted his options rather than expanded them.

Nick had been in commercial real estate for over twenty years, and during that time, his integrity, skill, and experience had earned him financial success and an excellent reputation among both colleagues and competitors. He'd been working for months on negotiating the close of several large neighboring properties when it occurred to him that once this transaction was complete, he had no other clients lined up on the horizon. Nick's logical business mind naturally began posing worrisome questions such as, Where is my next big project going to come from—and what if nothing comes? As the sole provider for his family, Nick believed that he needed to have plans A, B, C, and D in place for generating income and that he alone was responsible for formulating and executing those plans.

The thing to understand about Nick is that he is amazing at what he does. Confident, knowledgeable, and naturally charismatic, he has a flawless track record for delivering favorable outcomes for his clients. So while his talent was not in question, his next project was. Nick's brain kicked into high gear, spinning to come up with strategies for generating new business. He remembered events that he'd attended in years past that had resulted in beneficial introductions or lucrative referral sources, and he decided to spend some time researching similar events that he could attend in the near future.

As Nick shared this with me on our weekly coaching call, it was clear that none of the ideas he had generated lit him up, inspired him, or compelled him in any way to want to jump into action. They all felt like hard work, have-tos, and means to an end. I encouraged Nick to refrain from taking any immediate action and to focus instead on all the things he appreciated about himself, his career, and the positive impact he had made. He thought about all of the excellent results he'd produced for his clients over the years and felt appreciation for everyone he'd met in the process. He appreciated that his schedule was flexible and gave him the opportunity to earn a lot of money relatively quickly. He thought about the clients he had helped to get out of unfavorable situations and how satisfying it was to learn that their businesses had improved as a result. He recalled one particular charitable organization where he served on the board for three years, which enhanced his sense of community and provided meaningful ways to contribute his skills to those who otherwise wouldn't have access to them.

I explained to Nick that this internal practice of intentionally appreciating where he now stands and all that it took to get him here is actually a highly powerful and effective form of action. The action of appreciation generates internal momentum toward our ultimate result, and the more momentum we can generate prior to actually picking up the phone or calendaring a future event makes that result all the easier to come by.

I asked Nick to consider that all of the energy he'd offered over the course of his career has a life, or a momentum, of its own. All of the mental energy he'd invested in becoming better at his profession, and all the relief and happiness experienced by those he had helped with that knowledge, make up an energy stream that will continue to flow—into infinity. Remember that energy, once in motion, never dies. It only changes form. Ironically, the only thing that stops the flow of that energy from being a part of our experience is our anxiety that it may soon come to an end. But if we trust in the stream, if we trust in ourselves, if we appreciate the current of our good intentions that has carried us this far in the upward trajectory of our lives, it will lead us to every destination we want to go, without painstaking effort. The experience of paddling upstream is exhausting, but floating in the direction of a fast-moving current is bliss.

I asked Nick to try to imagine the energy of appreciation he was intentionally generating about himself and his career as a living, circulating force, radiating out into the universe ouching and subtly influencing everything it comes into contact with. I reminded him that much like the butterfly effect, which is the concept that even a small incident can trigger massive consequences, everything we do, say, or think has an impact on everyone and everything around us. Although Nick is a logical thinker and a practical businessman, he seemed satisfied and even comforted by this image, and he went back to completing the final details of his current project with a newfound sense of appreciation and a budding sense of trust. It wasn't his job to generate any new momentum, I assured him. He just had to acknowledge all the positive momentum he had already set into motion and allow himself to be carried on the stream of it.

Two days after our coaching session, Nick received a call from his twenty-four-year-old daughter, who had just returned from participating in a volunteer project in Mexico. The charitable organization that sponsored the project? You guessed it. It was run by the very same organization that Nick had served on the board for years earlier. Several of the members of the organization recognized Nick's daughter's last name, and they spent the bus ride home across the border telling her stories of how much positive change her dad had created during his time with them and how much they all liked and respected him. Later that same night, Nick received a text from one of the members. It turns out, the organization's lease was expiring in a few months and they had grown enough to justify purchasing property of their own. She couldn't think of anyone more qualified—or more knowledgeable about the organization's unique needs—to handle the purchase. In Nick's case, not taking immediate action in the face of a schedule opening was the most powerful action he could have possibly taken. It yielded far greater results than he ever achieved through advertising or attending networking functions.

If you find yourself contemplating an action that feels arduous or unpleasant, if you're feeling resistant about it rather than being carried on the wings of it, your best course of action is to back away from it. Delay moving the nonphysical energy of your desire into the external world of form until you have achieved a greater state of internal alignment. In every case, when you feel like the momentum is moving against you, your highest possible priority is to soften your internal struggle. Soothing your emotions before you take the action will save you the frustration of taking one step forward, two steps back.

By tuning in to your feelings, you'll be able to distinguish the vibration that is triggering your impulse to act. You can ask yourself questions: Is this action being motivated from a place of certainty or insecurity? Does it feel like the next logical step, or do I believe I have to overcompensate for something? Do I trust in my connection with this person, this project, this possibility, or am I trying to make something happen from a place of doubt or fear? Do I trust in my intentions and in the momentum I have already generated to date? Am I willing to be carried effortlessly and joyfully along the current of my desire, or do I feel compelled to control the current? If you discover that you're about to offer an action in order to compensate for energy that is misaligned, give yourself permission to walk away, to get a different perspective, or to think of something else.

The most effective course of action is to simply abandon the resistant thought. Abandon the activities that are getting you nowhere. Abandon your attachment to how your desire will be fulfilled, or the disappointment that it hasn't happened yet. Abandon the common-hour thinking of those who are still unaware of how manifestation really occurs, and allow yourself to place the majority of your focus on the alignment of energy. Once you're energetically aligned with the essence of what you desire, your next steps will look clearer and feel lighter and more logical. And, like Nick, you may be pleasantly surprised to discover that no external action from you is needed at all.

Balancing Internal and External Action

Anything that sets energy into motion is action. Whether it's physical energy, mental energy, or emotional energy—it's all energy, and therefore it's all action. Visualizing is taking action. Surrender, detachment, having faith, and feeling appreciation are all powerful forms of action. Picking up the phone, writing the email, having the conversation, joining the dating service, or applying for the job—these are actions too. And both types of actions, internal and external, are necessary.

The key to manifesting our desires is to take actions in accordance with the totality of who we are. We can't just approach it from the perspective that it's just our human self, our flesh suit, going through the motions and trying to make things happen. We have to invoke our nonphysical self and act in conjunction with the totality of

147

our energy and our connection to spirit. With every action, we can connect with the momentum of everything that came before and acknowledge that all of it—even the so-called missteps—was building up to our eventual manifestation. This marriage between inner alignment and outer momentum is what produces results that the world calls miraculous.

If there is a secret behind my ability to accomplish so much in so many different aspects of my life, it's that I make it a priority to first bring my internal energy into alignment with the essence of my desire *before* I take any external action. So when I'm with my kids, for example, my vibration is aligned with my intent that our relationship is harmonious, evolving, and fun. When I'm doing something that nurtures my body, I begin by connecting with my intention to fill myself with whatever vibration will serve me most at that moment—vitality, stamina, sexuality, relaxation, increased immunity, or whatever else will best serve me. When I'm working on a project or with students in a coaching program, the frequency that I offer is one of excitement and joyful anticipation, because I know that the best possible outcome for all concerned is now in the process of unfolding.

Even if you devote just one minute out of each hour to making sure your actions are aligned with your intent, the cumulative effect of this over time is staggering—and the results you produce will be far more effective. Marrying inner alignment with external action is the access point for tapping into that unseen reservoir known as intention. If you've ever heard accounts about human beings doing extraordinary and "impossible" things—like lifting a car to save a child or physically carrying someone to safety even though their body weighed two times their size—then you are already familiar with the power of intention. What most of us don't realize is that while times of great necessity (and great inspiration) draw this power to us naturally, we also have the ability to summon intention on purpose.

I was still working as a pharmaceutical sales rep when I was first introduced to the practice of combining inner intention with taking external action, and my job afforded me the perfect opportunity to field test this principle and find out how effective it really was. I had already noticed that anytime I brought the inner, or energetic, aspect into my work by deliberately offering a vibration that matched what I wanted to create, my success skyrocketed. So I conducted a little experiment: rather than making a certain number of sales calls each day and going out on appointments, all I did was meditate, visualize, intend, and allow. Not surprisingly, my sales numbers—which had been the highest in the district—fell to among the lowest. The following month, I combined the physical action of going out and making sales calls with the inner action of visualizing and feeling the success I wanted to create, and my numbers easily went right back up to the top. It's the combination of the two that is so powerful.

Some Law of Attraction experts I've met assert that creating internal alignment is more important than taking external action. My belief is that they are equally important. There is no magic pill. We can't just visualize what we want, slap a picture of it up on an altar, and bam, a new car will appear in the garage. Some degree of action is always required to bring about the fulfillment of any goal, but *inspired action*—which is the act of being energetically aligned with how we will feel once our goal is attained—is exponentially more powerful than action taken alone.

My husband, Frederic, is a golfer, and he recently explained to me that the perfect golf swing requires this balance between inner and outer action. It's equal parts envisioning where he wants the ball to go, quieting the chatter in his mind, and allowing his muscles to fire and his body to move instinctively, as a continuation of his mental alignment. In the same way Frederic can tee up a perfect golf shot, the universe has the ability to line up all the components needed for the manifestation of any desire, and it doesn't have to require hard work and excruciating amounts of action. We just have to line up with the end goal of what we want prior to moving toward it. Aligned action reflects a beautiful balance between doing and being—between summoning and allowing. And when alignment is present, positive momentum always ensues.

Generating Momentum toward Your Desire

You can choose to think of your desire from the perspective of it being out there ahead of you in time and space while you work your way to it. This is the path of uninspired action, and it is, by far, the long way around. Or you can choose instead to feel your desire as if it's already a part of your experience, because in actuality, it absolutely is! When you take this stance and wear your result like you would put on a suit and feel the luxury of the fabric, you gain access to information that's invisible to those who don't know about energy mastery. You can tap into this stream of inspiration right now by asking yourself: *What if I already was the type of person I am aspiring to be? What if I had already created the result I've been striving toward? And what are the actions that are naturally aligned with my result?* These questions open you up to possibility thinking, speeding the momentum toward your desire.

Watch those who are right now living the experiences that you desire, and you'll see that their energy is absolutely aligned in this area of their lives. People who are good with money, for example, demonstrate respect for it. People in happy intimate relationships prioritize those relationships and show up for their partners intentionally, not sloppily. With any result that you wish to create—whether it's a successful business or a thriving physical body—allow yourself to see the actions, both internal and external, that will support and sustain that creation. For example, if you desire a new car, begin treating your current car the way you imagine you'll treat the new one. If you're seeking a job promotion, dress the part now. Powerfully decide to promote yourself to a new level of self-confidence, self-respect, and self-worth.

If you had already created all that you desire, what are the actions you would take on a regular basis to keep that momentum going? Some people think that the joy of manifestation lies in finally having the freedom to rest on our laurels and do nothing, but I guarantee you this is not the case. The greatest joy in the process of creation is getting to participate with that which you have created. Remember that creation is governed by the Law of Attraction. You are intentionally developing a love affair with your desire, so think of it with the same fondness as you would think of a lover!

Our desires gather momentum in the presence of acknowledgment, praise, trust, belief, and appreciation, and their power is diffused anytime we introduce judgment, criticism, or doubt into the equation. In a culture in which we've been taught that the way to guarantee success and positive change is through railing against the status quo, it is vital to remember that every desire unfolds along its own path, according to its own timeframe. The manifestation of your desires unfolds easily when you are soft and pliable, in an open and receptive state of being.

To build positive momentum, our only work is to define what we want and to then think, speak, and feel ourselves into having it. It's to contemplate often about all the ways our desire thrills us and all the things we anticipate learning and experiencing along the way of its becoming. It's to speak in favor of our desire, never against it. Like a golfer or any other athlete warms up before hitting the course or stepping onto the field, we need to prepare ourselves vibrationally before we ever step into action. Our efforts are infinitely more effective when we warm ourselves up ahead of time. If we apply effort while we're feeling cold and unprepared, we siphon all the manifestation magic out of the moment.

Think of it this way: Would you expect to enjoy a great meal if you weren't hungry? Would you expect to have a fantastic time with your partner if you'd spent the day rehashing all the complaints you've ever had about him over the years? Would you expect to do well on a five-mile run if you hadn't stretched out ahead of time? Of course you wouldn't. You would give yourself the best opportunity to succeed by warming up to whatever activity you were about to engage in. I'm asking you to do the same thing with the energy of your moods, your emotions, your expectations, and your thoughts.

Prior to sitting down at your desk to work, mentally rehearse everything you love about your job. Make a mental list of all your talents and past successes. Think about the positive aspects of the project you're working on. Prepare your internal environment for an effortless, easy, exhilarating experience. When the universe throws you the ball, so to speak, you have to be both willing and ready to catch it. And this means positioning yourself in the most advantageous stance ahead of time. Train yourself in advance. Believe in your abilities. Reminisce about past successes. Visualize what you want to unfold and how you believe you will feel. These inner actions are powerful. They open a space for the universe to rush in and do the rest, and then we easily accomplish the things we desire.

This is the magical way that life is meant to unfold for each of us, all the time. And we can take comfort in the fact that even in its perfection, this process is never complete, for the moment a desire is realized, a new one is born from that very experience. Desire is the launching point of all new creation.

Chapter 7: The Principle of Action— Applying It Step by Step

---

1 When you consider your current Desire Factor, notice whether you typically feel more negative or positive momentum. Do you most frequently feel like you are moving forward with ease, standing still, or backsliding?

2 What thoughts, attitudes, and actions might help you to reverse any negative momentum and come back into more neutrality and alignment?

3 During those times when you feel in perfect alignment with your desire, what types of inspiration naturally arise within you? What is the nature of the thoughts you think? What positive actions are you inspired to take?

4 Build on your desire's positive momentum from a state of neutrality and receptivity. The following process will support you in doing this.

Energy Mastery Exercise

Balancing the Forces of Alignment and Momentum

*B*egin by taking a moment to situate yourself in a place where you can give your time and attention completely to yourself. Turn off your phone, and make sure there are no distractions around you. Just declare this next segment of time as totally your own, as an opportunity to more harmoniously align with the object of your desire.

And when you're ready, go ahead and close your eyes, taking a couple of slow, deep, delicious breaths and allowing yourself to completely release and relax with each exhale. Allow your attention to gradually withdraw from the outer world of form and function and to return home to your inner world of feeling and vibration.

Begin to mentally review each of the principles we've explored throughout this book—the Principles of Alignment, Focus, Joyful Expectancy, Having, Loving, Surrender, and Action. And as you reflect on each one, acknowledge that every step of deliberate creation involves action on our part. What you are doing right now—taking time out of your external life to acknowledge the inner stream of energy that sustains all things—is a powerful form of action. Take a moment to appreciate yourself for doing this important inner work of alignment.

And with your next deep breath, bring to mind once more the object of your desire. See the image of it, feel the feelings you associate with its fulfillment, and allow yourself to begin to attune in body, mind, and heart with the vibration of it. Acknowledge that all of your heartfelt desires come forth from a divine source and that your only job is to allow them into being. Feel your source energy flowing through you with greater momentum and velocity— lighting your path, bringing you into greater alignment with your Desire Factor, and effortlessly guiding your actions.

And now, feeling your energetic connection with the fulfillment of your desire, allow yourself to see what actions you could take today—and take to the very best of your ability—to move closer to its fulfillment. What part are you—as a physical expression of infinite, nonphysical, divine source energy—being asked to take in order to make manifest your heart's desire?

Give yourself permission to follow these instructions, to follow through on the flow and inspiration of each impulse you receive. Every clue is a vital link in a chain reaction that will result in the total fulfillment of your desires.

Remember that you are never alone in anything that you desire to create. The Divine is always backing you up, and your inner guidance is always pointing you toward that infinite reservoir of wisdom. See yourself moving into each action as a powerful cocreator with the Divine. Remember to fill yourself up first with the energy of already having, being, and living what you love and desire. Listen to the inner guidance you receive, and take the actions you are being called to take to the very best of your ability.

As you begin to return your awareness back to the room that you're in, take a slow deep breath in, and let it out, allowing yourself to become more aware of your physical surroundings. Taking another deep breath in and letting it out, begin to wiggle your fingers and toes, slowly coming back, and when you are ready, gently open up your eyes. Give yourself a moment to take a nice stretch and to notice any subtle shifts that you can feel within your body.

CONCLUSION

It Was Never about the Desire

Since this has been a book about deliberately manifesting your heart's desires, it would be easy, and logical, to assume that its effectiveness could be measured by the number of desires that the philosophies and practices outlined here have helped you to manifest. If this were the case, you could give yourself a gold star for the new car in the garage, for the increase in income you've attracted, or for the jeans that now zip up a little easier than they did a few weeks ago. But the real value of what has been presented throughout this book goes much deeper than any of that.

The act of bringing your desires into full physical manifestation is a huge part of your three-dimensional experience. It's natural for you—as the furthest extension of the source energy that creates and sustains everything in this universe—to want to transform invisible, nonphysical vibration into physical, tangible things. The larger, infinite, Divine Self that you truly are is continually transmitting its signal to you, like an umbilical cord connecting the nonphysical to the physical. You receive this energy transmission as an idea or an impulse, and as that impulse gathers speed, it takes root in your consciousness as a desire. There is something so deliciously exhilarating about watching a fledgling desire mature into the full realization of all that you knew it had the potential to be. And it's thrilling to recognize yourself as an active, deliberate participant in the process of its creation and to acknowledge each of the steps you took along the way.

This cocreative dance begins with you becoming aware of something that you perceive as missing. Maybe it's a reality you've seen others enjoying that you want to experience for yourself. Or something perhaps that feels unattainable or out of reach. Your Desire Factor seems far away or separate from you, but you still feel it vibrating within you. Eventually you have to acknowledge that it's too strong to ignore, even if you have no idea how you're going to pull it off.

Then you begin the process of mentally, emotionally, and energetically warming up to that desire. You align yourself with the broader part of you, which knows you are divinely designed for wholeness, health, and well-being. This leads you to experience abundance in all aspects, including financial prosperity. You enjoy creative self-expression that leads to success and loving and supportive relationships. And you acknowledge that alignment—more than hard work or meticulous planning—is the mechanism through which the most joyful manifestations occur.

You then use your incredible power of focus to generate and enhance the feeling within you of already being one with the object of your desire. You accept it as a reality that already exists, and joyfully anticipate its further manifestation into your life. You deliberately conjure what it will feel like to have the presence of your desire, and in doing so, bring yourself into greater vibrational harmony with the experiences and outcomes you want to attract. You acknowledge that your relationship with this new and expanded reality began the moment you first conceived of it, and you flow your loving energy and appreciation toward that relationship, even though it's still very much in the process of becoming.

Gradually, you learn to interact with your desire unconditionally—surrendering your attachment of how or when or through which avenue it will unfold—and trust in the process itself. And then, as you are so inspired, you allow yourself to be called into actions that further align you with the joyful expansion that underlies every desire.

In granting your desire permission to live within you and to move through you, you are in conscious communion with the energy that creates and sustains all things. Once this energy stream has been summoned and allowed by you, it cannot not continue to flow. Like a wave moves steadily toward the shoreline, the energy of desire, once summoned, seeks manifestation in physical form. Sometimes the form it manifests into is drastically different than what we originally conceived, but it's the energy itself moving through us that is life-giving. Who we become in the process of receiving, aligning with, and acting in accordance with our desires is the real manifestation we're all seeking. I experienced a deeply personal reminder of this while in the process of writing this book.

One night many years ago when my family and I were visiting Montreal, Frederic was flipping through the only two English-broadcasting TV stations and came across a new game show called *Beat Shazam*, hosted by Jamie Foxx, whom I have always loved and admired as a comedian and actor. The show was based around music trivia, which was right up my alley and

so fun. Even more fun was the fact that I consistently called out the right answers to the song titles, as if the selection of music had been a soundtrack from my own life. Surprised by my knowledge of music, my boys told me that I should apply to be a contestant on the show, and Frederic chimed in that because of all my media experience, I would do great. With that, a tiny seed of desire planted itself in my consciousness.

After we returned home, the next season of the show started, and every week our family would get together to watch. I loved experiencing this show together. Jamie Foxx was so funny and entertaining, and I continued to know most of the answers to the trivia questions. Once again my boys encouraged me, "Mom, you really need to go on this show," and Frederic agreed. I downloaded the Shazam app and started playing along with the show from the app and continued to do pretty well.

During the show's third season, I acknowledged that I truly did have a desire to be a contestant, so I took a logical and inspired action. I reached out to my PR person to find out how to go about arranging an audition. They had finished filming the third season, but my publicist sent me a link to complete an online application for the upcoming season, which I did. The show selects contestants who are partnered in pairs, and so, after submitting the video, I immediately thought of partnering with my friend Natalie, who is also a huge fan of music. I let her know what I was up to, and even though she had never watched the show, Natalie—who is always game for a good challenge—rallied and was willing to play.

Months went by, and frankly I didn't even think about the application I had submitted until one day the following January when I was called by the casting agent for *Beat Shazam*. I was beyond excited and texted Natalie right away to give her the news, and she was like, "Oh God . . ." not sure what I had gotten her into.

I was so tuned in to the presence and power within me, I had no doubt that this desire had been divinely inspired. I knew this because of the excitement I felt when I thought about it. I was sure the reason I was experiencing this desire was because the Divine wanted to experience it through me. So I made a decision that I would do anything I was asked to do in order to cooperate with its unfolding. I accepted it as happening, and when I was asked to audition over Skype, I happily agreed.

I did everything I knew to do to set myself up for success. I got my hair and makeup professionally done. I set my computer up with perfect lighting. I was diligent about practicing the song titles while listening to the radio, while working out, and in every other free moment in which I could test my knowledge. I even downloaded a couple of music trivia apps and would play them several times throughout the day. Every night before bed, I would connect with my Divine Self and feel the deep connection. I saw myself as a contestant on *Beat Shazam* and winning the million-dollar prize. In my mind's eye, I imagined a white screen on which the words "I choose . . ." were written, with lines following the words as if on a ruled tablet. I saw myself filling in the blank spaces in my own handwriting—"I choose to win one million dollars on *Beat Shazam*"—and then focused on the power of each word.

I accepted the fulfillment of this desire with all of my being, feeling it as if it had already happened. I felt the expansion of success, the expansion of freedom.

Every night I would ask myself why I wanted to be on the show and what I would do with the million dollars once I'd won it, and then I mentally made a list of all the reasons. I wanted to show my boys that it is possible to be, do, or have anything that we desire. I wanted to have extra money to invest into my business so that my coaching could have a positive impact on even more people. I wanted to take my husband on an extravagant cruise for his fiftieth birthday. I wanted to give more generously to several organizations committed to ending hunger both in Arizona and in Africa. I wanted to meet Jamie Foxx and thank him for how much joy he has brought to my life. More than anything, I wanted to experience the exhilaration and the fun that I associated with this manifestation. Clear about all the *whys*, I would then see myself on the show being joyous, happy, loving, and free, and I would flow love to every part of what I was seeing. I would then speak out

loud, "It is done." And then I would surrender the desire and all the energy connected to it to my Divine Self. I'd let go and let the Divine flow as I got out of the way.

The first audition was a blast. I did really well, and so did Natalie. They immediately put us through to the next round of online auditions and asked us a few questions about ourselves. A few days later I was contacted by the casting director, who asked me if I could audition again—this time with someone in the same room—because Natalie was in LA while I was in Scottsdale. I asked Frederic to fill in, and he was happy to do it, so we set up the next round of auditions.

He and I did great, and the experience, again, was so much fun. The casting director loved our energy and our chemistry, so much so that she asked us to fill out a long-form application and send along several photos of us as a couple. We immediately filled it out with great enthusiasm. The stage was set for the producers to pitch us to the network.

They informed us of the show's taping dates, which happened to be the same weekend as a couple's retreat that Frederic and I were scheduled to facilitate. So we decided to cancel the couple's retreat in order to make ourselves available. And we continued to practice, and I continued to feel my way into the manifestation of this desire.

Then I was contacted again by the casting agent, who said they wanted to have me audition with another woman who was also a wife and mom. I thought of my friend Bobette, a spunky DJ who I often hire for my local events. I reached out to her, and she was excited and eager to participate. I asked the casting agent if they were still considering having Frederic and me on the show, and she said yes, explaining that they simply wanted another option based on what they were looking for. Each show has three teams of two people, and they were looking for specific relationships within these teams.

Because this was now my third audition, the casting director already knew me. Bobette and I showed up for our online audition, hair and makeup ready, 100 percent committed to being on the show and doing the best we could to solidify our chances. We did great, and the casting director called me back that day and wanted us to audition again. So a couple of days later, Bobette and I got back on a Skype call and were quizzed on the music as well as asked some different questions about our relationship with music, how we knew each other, and why we wanted to be on the show.

I of course had my answers ready because I had rehearsed them in my head thousands of times. I felt so grateful for this experience and the fun I was having. And while they did not ask Bobette and me to fill out the long-form application, the chances of getting on the show with Frederic were still really great. I was 100 percent sure I would make it to the show. I felt this as an already-achieved outcome, and more importantly I felt the ways this desire was continuing to inspire and expand me.

During this time my life started to expand in ways I could never have expected or imagined. My husband and I started a new business that magically came together. After getting some blood work done for life insurance I discovered that my health was better at forty-nine than it had been at any previous time in my life. I felt unstoppable. I felt in the flow. I felt so grateful for all that had manifested, all that was manifesting, and all that was about to manifest.

The taping dates for *Beat Shazam* were fast approaching, and I still hadn't received confirmation whether I would be on the show. Like Tom Petty says, the waiting for the manifestation to happen is the hardest part. And we really only have two choices. We can either keep our faith moving in the direction of what we want or give in to our fears of what we don't want. So I kept the faith. I reached out to both the casting agents, one via Skype and the other by text.

The one that I was texting with told me, "At this point if you'd been chosen I think someone would have reached out." And I went into complete disappointment and sadness.

I felt devastated. I felt like the universe, God, the Divine, my angels . . . everyone and everything had abandoned me. I wanted to throw everything out and quit. I couldn't believe how everything I know about universal laws could fail me, or maybe it was me who had failed to correctly work the laws. I couldn't understand how the journey of making my way through all four auditions—which I had nailed and which were so fun and exciting and flowing with energy—could lead to absolutely nothing. I allowed myself to feel my emotions, because when a desire does not manifest in the way we have asked for and causes a future projection to shift, we are naturally left with a feeling of loneliness, separation, and abandonment and an inclination to simply give up.

Knowing that the key to releasing these resistant emotions is to process them and allow them to move through me, I had a couple of good cries. Once on my way to the grocery store, I parked my car under a tree, and the tears just flowed. I felt every emotion—anger, disappointment, frustration, confusion, sadness, despair, grief, and fear. Later in the day, I took a shower, and the tears came and came until there were no more.

I then reached out to the casting agent who had originally auditioned me. She was the one who had asked me to audition a second time and who'd directed Frederic and me to fill out the long-form application, which we promptly did when asked.

I messaged her: "Hi, Heidi. I have been looking for updates on casting for *Beat Shazam* on the social media sites. I just want to make sure I haven't missed anything. Should I assume that we were not chosen if we haven't heard anything at this point? Thanks;)"

Her reply? "Hi Christy! Final decisions will be made by the first week of March."

What? All the information I had received up to this point was that taping would begin on February 28 and casting decisions would be made well in advance of that. Despite appearances, the possibility that this very specific desire would manifest in the way I had envisioned it was still very much alive. I was grateful that I had processed all the resistance that I was feeling and had moved back into feeling expanded by—rather than defeated by—my desire. I surrendered to this new development and continued to wait.

During this waiting time, I was invited to my son Alex's school to watch him give a speech. Afterward, I had a couple of free hours before I would return to pick up Alex and his brother from school that day, so I called my parents. They were at a nearby restaurant, and I joined them for lunch. My mom was talking about a friend

of hers who, despite having much to be grateful for, can usually be found voicing some kind of complaint. "She cries with a loaf of bread under her arm," my mom said of her friend. My mom has lots of quirky sayings, which I have teased her about my entire life, but I had never heard this one before, and it really struck me.

I suddenly realized how many loaves of bread I have—meaning just how much I have to be grateful for. It was clear that my desire to be on *Beat Shazam* was causing me to expand in yet another important way. I needed to learn to stay in gratitude no matter what the outcome was. So I was prepared to be called but also prepared that it might not happen, and if it didn't, that was okay.

The new taping dates came and went, and I never did hear back. But what I now understood was that while my Desire Factor did not manifest into the particular form I had envisioned, the energy summoned by the desire was still flowing strong and was expressing itself in many different ways in my life. In fact, virtually every other aspect of my life—including my business, my marriage, my family, and my health—was vibrating at a higher level of success than ever before. And this, I knew, was as a direct result of the life-giving energy that the desire to participate on *Beat Shazam* had summoned through me.

The Council shared with me that the energy that I had flowed toward this desire had not gone unnoticed, nor was it wasted. They explained that the fact that I never manifested being on the show doesn't matter. What matters is who I became in the process of allowing myself to lean in the direction of that desire and to embrace it fully. Because of that, I am vibrating at a much higher level, and so much more abundance is flowing through me and around me. I understand more than I ever have what it means to surrender to the universe's plan for my life.

The old saying that having a plan is a sure way to make God laugh really applies here, because the fact is, there is only so much

of the horizon that we can see with our human eyes or ponder with our human brains. How many times have you had the experience of something you wanted not working out—the guy never called back, the potential client decided to go a different route, the escrow fell through—only to later realize that this so-called setback was a pivotal step along the path to something much better? The joy in life is not to identify a desire and then systematically set about accomplishing it, like checking an item off your to-do list. The joy is to allow yourself to be carried along its energy stream, even when you have no idea where it's taking you, and then discover that it was you, your Divine Self, that set this current into motion.

If you stay pointed in the direction of this energy stream, and don't allow the changing landmarks along the way to pull you off track, if you remain obedient to the call of source and place your inner alignment with that above all external things, the energy will carry you in the direction of joyful expansion—even if you don't arrive at the precise destination your human mind has decided you're supposed to go.

I was hesitant to share this story here because the way my human brain had orchestrated things, I would go on the show, win the million dollars, connect with Jamie Foxx, go on *Oprah*, eradicate hunger, change the world . . . and none of those things manifested. So one might think that I was not a success (I certainly did at first). But the gift of the Desire Factor is not the actual manifestation; it is the flow of energy that is summoned through us in every act of wanting. I think most people in personal development would tell you that it's really about the result, the accomplishment, or the success that we manifest into a particular physical form. And it certainly is true that it's the human part of us that fuels our attachment to the actual form. But when we surrender and look at who we became in the process of embracing any heartfelt desire, we see that we are more than we ever were before because of it.

As this new understanding settled within me, I witnessed several of my coaching clients put their Desire Factor in motion toward something that didn't end up manifesting exactly the way they wanted it to, and I saw how other aspects of their lives were expanding and unfolding in amazing, joyful ways. The contrast of what we don't want gives way to more of what we do want, which gives way to another desire. And on and on it goes.

At the time of this writing, the Desire Factor to be a part of *Beat Shazam* is still alive and well within me, so I applied for the next season. I contacted my best friend Alesa, who is a wife and mother and also loves music, and invited her to audition as my partner. She is excited by the idea, and—after putting in the application with her—I can feel the flow of the desire start moving again. As far as where this desire will take me, I'm in total surrender, because ultimately it is the life-giving flow of the energy of the Divine that I really want to experience.

The most amazing thing is that the Divine individualized itself as me, as you, even before we ever came forth as distinct units of consciousness. In order for you and I to exist, the divine mind had to conceive of you, focus you into being, and this focus of energy was the beginning of the individualizing process, out of which you and I manifested in physical form. We are the Desire Factor that is born in the mind of the Divine.

So I encourage you to practice the seven principles that we've explored together throughout this book. They will never lead you astray, even if they lead you to a destination other than the one you have planned. Remember that you are the magnificent spirit that chose this body and this lifetime in order to enjoy everything that life has to offer, knowing that all of it would expand your awareness of the broader part of you, and that all roads would lead you back home to the immense spiritual power of yourself.

Resources

Christy Whitman and the Quantum Council offer many additional resources to help you implement the information in *The Desire Factor.*

- 30 Days of Quantum Success Meditations: www.christy whitman.com/quantumsuccess

- Quantum Energy Mastery: www.quantumenergymastery .com

- Quantum Success Coaching Academy: www.quantum -success-coaching-academy.com

And to download and implement the information from *The Desire Factor* visit www.thedesirefactor.com/action and join the seven-week course called The Desire Factor in Action with Christy & the Council.

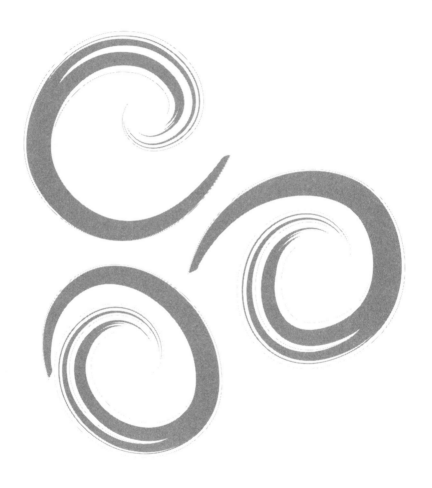

Acknowledgments

I first want to acknowledge my new home, my publisher Beyond Words, and all the people who cared for this baby. Being a published author for twenty years, this has by far been my best and most supportive experience. I truly feel I have a family who understands and gets me. Thank you.

I want to thank my literary agent, Devra Jacobs, whose introduction story is outlined in this book. Truly a Desire Factor.

I want to acknowledge Marianne Williamson as one of my first spiritual teachers. After I wrote my first book my Desire Factor was to have Marianne endorse my book. After six books, that Desire Factor came to fruition. Thank you, Marianne.

I want to acknowledge and thank all the people on my team that support me in what I do. Danielle Dorman as my editor, you are beyond lady! Beth Myers, truly the best assistant I have ever had. Terri Romine, we still are growing together and have been for fourteen years. Tabitha, aka "Tabulous," you really are a divine send! Kim Gore, go get 'em gal! Nada Howarth, Sheila Callaham, and Barbara Anselmi . . . thank you to my entire team.

I want to thank my sister in light, Christina Hill, for helping me expand into light and for collaborating with me in The Healing Room to help so many people find their way back to light.

To Athella . . . there are no words, just energy of gratitude.

To the Council, you feel me. Thank you for changing my life, and for transforming so many of our clients' lives.

To my parents that I am so deeply grateful for . . . thank you for showing me the contrast so I could have the clarity in my own life.

And to you the reader. You have been calling this information forth from your own contrast, clarity, and intentions. This is for you with great appreciation for your growth.

About the Author

*C*hristy Whitman is a transformational leader, celebrity coach, and Law of Attraction expert, as well as the two-time *New York Times* bestselling author of *The Art of Having It All, Taming Your Alpha Bitch*, and international bestseller *Quantum Success*.

Christy has appeared on media outlets, including *The Today Show, The Morning Show,* TEDx, and the Hallmark Channel. She and her work have been featured in various publications, including Goalcast, *People, Seventeen, Woman's Day*, Hollywood Life, and *Teen Vogue*, to name a few.

Christy is the CEO and founder of the Quantum Success Coaching Academy, a ten-month Law of Attraction coaching certification program. She has helped certify over three thousand life coaches and has helped countless others to unlock their power to manifest. Christy is also the channel for a group of ascended masters who call themselves the Quantum Council of Light, or "the Council."